Unbelievable!

How to Hypnotically Shift *Any* Conversation
and Instantly Capture Attention—Using
One Magic Word.

Robert Martel

Advanced Praise for *Unbelievable:*

"You've always wanted to be more successful, but you just don't know how. With this book, *Unbelievable* by Bob Martel, you will be able to positively influence every conversation in therapy, in business, and in your personal life. People will listen and follow your lead because they believe what you say is true. More importantly, Bob's wisdom will provoke change from within, and the results will be astounding. This book shows the power of one single word that can change almost anything! It's a must-read for anyone who wants to succeed in business or life!"

—Dr. Richard Nongard, author of *The Seven Most Effective Methods of Self-Hypnosis*

"Martel has done it again! Turned my world inside out in just the way he can. He's incredible! No, better said, 'unbelievable!' I have always heard the word unbelievable as a negative. Thanks to Martel, I have a choice, one I enjoy making. If you are like me, this book will make a change in your life."

—Joseph Onesta, clinical hypnotist, author of *Life Without Diabetes* and *Deleting Diabetes*

"What would it mean for your life if you could unlock the secret to being more influential? Bob Martel shares an unbelievably simple approach to being more influential in business, your personal life, even with your clients. In this engaging book, you'll learn simple ways to transform yourself. Because of those positive changes, you'll see better results in all facets of life. The stories and examples in this book are relatable and easy to understand. If you're looking for actionable ideas that can lead to quick results, you have to read this book."

—Christopher Leier, author of *The Magic of No*

"Believe it! Bob Martel is the real deal when it comes to hypnosis and transformation. Capturing attention in a day and age of distraction is a skill and an art. Learn from a master. This book really is *unbelievable!*"

—Joanne McCall, author of *Media Darling*

"Unbelievable! Bob Martel is a master at how to influence others in subtle ways to create major changes either in yourself or others! This is a book you need to read if you want to influence anyone in your life and give yourself the confidence you need to enter all situations. Reading this will change your trajectory in the right direction."

—James M. Vera, author of *Three Powerful Words: The Secret Affirmation That Unlocks Everything*

"Once again, Robert Martel has created a book so simple and practical to use. This book will help you in ALL your varied relationships in life.

Robert has mastered the proactive use of language for the betterment of all who use it. At first glance, you may wonder how the use of a single word or two can change the dynamics of a conversation. Well, just think of how you felt when someone told you that they loved you or maybe something not so kind. Your state can immediately change based on the use of a simple word. These are power words: words not used regularly in our conversations that interrupt a person's normal perception and then causes them to pay attention to what was just said. This simple technique can be used in sales, business, negotiations, and perhaps most importantly, your personal relationships. I highly recommend this book. Buy it and use it!"

—Thomas Roman CHT, The Quantum Group

"This book is "unbelievably" spot on. Many great tidbits on how to increase your powers to influence. Exchanging the old adage of needing to "See it to believe it," Bob has highlighted the newer, better paradigm of first believing it to see results. This should be mandatory reading for all who are looking for that extra advantage in life."

—Karen Dubi, life coach at Flexible Mindset Strategies, author of *The Art of Getting Out of Your Own Way*

Also by Robert Martel

*How to Create All of the Business
You Can Handle*

The Magic of Aesop

I Am Sleeping Now

Unbelievable!

How to Hypnotically Shift *Any* Conversation
and Instantly Capture Attention—Using
One Magic Word.

Robert Martel

Unbelievable: How to Hypnotically Shift *Any* Conversation and Instantly Capture Attention—Using *One* Magic Word.

ISBN: 978-1-7354770-3-9

First printing February 2023

Positive Results Hypnosis

www.positiveresultshypnosis.com

www.anunbelievablebook.com

Cover Design by Pankaj Singh Renu

Disclaimer: The author is not responsible for the positive changes and excitement that lie ahead in your life as a result of implementing any of the advice offered within these pages. Proceed at your own risk in using the word *unbelievable* to capture attention, sharpen your charismatic skills, or otherwise influence others. Enjoy the unbelievable results you will start to see over the course of your lifetime, beginning today, as you take a chance by adding this word to your repertoire and inject your unbelievable self into the conversation.

www.bobmartel.com

For Lori, who has been an unbelievable addition to my life.

Introduction

Ever struggle to jump into the conversation or simply wish to be heard?

Using the word *unbelievable* will help you establish focused attention quickly.

Ever wish you could command attention and let your voice, your opinions, and ideas be understood? Ever search for that attention-getting word that delivers high impact or an idea that would capture the attention of all whose ears heard what you had to say?

Stand by.

Things are going to start changing and quickly, too, for the better!

Imagine you, unbelievable. Own that notion because it's true!

In fact, no matter how you feel about yourself at this very moment, pause and say, "I am unbelievable." Three more times now, then keep reading!

Imagine the unbelievable conversational that takes place when you take command of the dialogue, magnetically attracting attention.

Conceive it. Believe it. Achieve it!

This one word, *unbelievable*, gives you the courage to think, act, and be the very person you want to be and feel the feelings of positivity that emerge from your thinking it, saying it, hearing it, and adopting it.

It's *unbelievable* how one word can transform your life or make such an impression to others. This one magic word will do the trick!

"Believe you can, and you're halfway there." —Theodore Roosevelt

To be sure, you are quite likely familiar with the phrase; *I'll believe it when I see it.* The reverse can be true as well. *When I believe it, I'll see it (and feel it). And when I feel it in my unbelievably imaginative mind first, I can then begin to move toward it to make my intention real.*

If you have struggled to deliver true impact when you are speaking to a group or to an individual, be it at home, in the workplace, or even at a restaurant, ticket counter, or wherever you may be, then you'll be anxious to test-drive what you learn in this book. Imagine, with one spoken word, you can help your listeners to instantly feel what you have seen and felt—to some degree, at least.

It may seem a bit unbelievable at this moment, but this *one word* seems to instantly hypnotize just about everyone, and it commands equally rapid attention.

You just (re)discovered it in the previous sentence, and well, I suppose it's quite evident right there in the title: *Unbelievable.* You are about to discover or be reminded that this seemingly innocuous word wields so much power when used with skill and finesse.

The word was drilled into me at a sales training super conference at the then brand-new Boston Garden or Fleet Center, the new home of the Bruins and the Celtics. That was the early nineties. Zig Ziglar. Dan Kennedy. Larry King. Barbara Bush was followed by Tom Hopkins, the famous sales trainer and motivational speaker.

Hopkins is the author of How to Master the Art of Selling, in which he talks about using the word with precision in sales situation, yet it has so much more applicability. And when you pause to think about it, we are all—each one of us—in sales at some level as influencers and persuaders. Experimenting with power words is, well, unbelievably fun and even profitable, and truth be told, I had used the hypnotic word much earlier.

So flashback further. It's October 1973. Disneyworld had opened two years earlier. Yours truly and some Navy buddies were roaming the grounds on liberty from boot camp for the day in our white sailor suits, no less. It is still an unbelievable memory. Lots of fun, especially because of that uniform. Couldn't buy a drink. But I did use the word unbelievable to buy a drink for one of the Disney patrons. "Hey," I said, "you look unbelievable," and without a pause, "Will you let this sailor buy you a drink?" Worked. But I was never sure if it was the phrase or the uniform. You always have to factor in the nonverbal cues when communicating.

****

Words matter, you know that, so you'll relate to this sage advice from the *Maxims of Ptahhotep*, who was a vizier or prime minister in today's vernacular, serving the Pharoah in the Fifth Dynasty under Pharoah Djedkare Isesi in 2500 BC:

> *That you may be strong, be a Craftsman in speech; for the strength of one is the tongue and the speech of one is mightier than all fighting.*

—Ptahhotep,
The Scribe of Saqqara, Egypt, 2500 BC

But I digress.

Thanks for indulging me on that brief historical side road. I wanted to share Ptahhotep's quote from his book, considered the oldest book in the world. Sage advice indeed! As Ptahhotep would advise you today, sharpen your tongue with influential words. Reread Ptahhotep's words above. Decide now to improve your word mastery to influence the world around you.

I wonder, though, whether Ptahhotep's eloquence and wisdom influenced the stories told by Aesop in his famous fables. We know Aesop's Fables influenced (and continue to influence) the world. Food for thought but a digression.

Adding the word *unbelievable* to your repertoire with great skill and timing will transform your way of thinking and how you experience the world around you. More importantly, it will change how you feel—about yourself and about others!

When you think about it, it really is unbelievable, isn't it?

The word magically stops people in their tracks, and if they are even the slightest engaged, it will spark their curiosity about what you really mean or what's coming next.

Here's what you should expect:

You are going to discover that the word *unbelievable* is going to create change for you, including:

- Be the person you want to be, whom God wants you to be
- Be that person who commands attention when you speak
- Instantly enhance your self-image
- Chart a new course in your life
- See the world differently through new eyes
- Shift your perspective on any issue
- Laugh at the world and at yourself
- Feel more in control
- Reconnect with your authenticity
- Change your world and the world around you
- Influence how others see you by your confidence

- Increase your courage, confidence, and charisma
- Skyrocket your self-esteem and self-worthiness
- Jump-start a new journey
- Command attention and take control of any conversation

Get Ready to Achieve *Unbelievable* Results in Your Everyday and Professional Communications

Family and Friends: Good communication is essential in any relationship. It helps to build trust, understanding, and mutual respect. Listening carefully to what your family and friends are saying can help you resolve conflicts more quickly and maintain a strong bond between all of you. Clear communication also helps foster healthy relationships that last a lifetime.

In the Workplace: Effective communication is essential in today's workplace. It helps to boost productivity, increase morale, and ensure everyone is on the same page with projects or tasks they are working on together. Good communication skills help employees understand instructions and expectations more clearly, allowing them to work better as a team.

Public Speaking and Meetings: The ability to speak confidently in front of an audience is essential for any professional. Knowing how to craft a good message and deliver it effectively can make all the difference when trying to get your point across or persuade others. Whether giving a presentation, speaking at a meeting, or participating in a debate, good communication skills are paramount.

Daily Life on the Street: Communication is just as important in everyday life. Whether you're talking to a store clerk, asking directions on the street, or interacting with people in other public settings, having good communication skills will help ensure that your interactions go smoothly and are successful.

In Selling Yourself or Your Products and Services: Selling yourself or your products and services requires excellent communication skills. You must be able to convey the value of what you are selling in a clear, concise manner that resonates with potential customers or clients. Being able to listen carefully and understand customer needs is also important so that you can tailor your sales pitch according to their individual wants and needs.

In Social Media: With the rise of social media, communication is becoming increasingly digital. Knowing how to craft a good message in the limited character space of social media sites like Twitter and Instagram can be tricky. Good communication skills are essential for getting your point across and connecting with others online. Additionally, being able to listen carefully to what people are saying and responding appropriately is essential for avoiding conflict and maintaining positive relationships online.

Why Keep Reading This Book?

There are two reasons to keep reading, to be sure.

First of all, I've written this book to call your attention to a word that belongs in your "influence arsenal," and secondly, I wrote it for a little lighthearted fun for you to add to your daily conversations. As you play with this word in your daily life and watch people's responses, you'll certainly have a few chuckles. If you are really observant, you'll notice with great awareness how people seem to gravitate toward you. They want to know what comes next when you utter *unbelievable* in any conversation.

The word *unbelievable*, used properly, creates amazing instant rapport and charisma!

My hope for you and my very goal is that before you even turn the page, your mind is serving up a few ways you'll use the word to start getting new reactions from people. Play with it. Use it strategically. Use it to relax people who may be expecting a different word or reaction from you. Weave it into your vocabulary without overuse and anticipate new behavioral responses. Have fun with it, and watch the word take your life to new places. Brace yourself for an unbelievable response.

Use it gingerly at first, and make it roll off your tongue naturally. Overuse will create an adverse effect.

Remember these unbelievable pearls of wisdom below and read on!

> *Seeing is believing, but feeling is the truth.* And *'Tis skill, not strength, that governs a ship.*
>
> —Thomas Fuller, British scholar, preacher, and one of the most witty and prolific authors of the seventeenth century.

Use your new mastery of the word *unbelievable* in your conversations and help others feel the impact of your words and steer their own ships as a result. Lofty? Perhaps, but entirely possible, if you'll only believe it! Strengthen those skills.

This is important.

Keep this in mind: No matter how lightly or how deeply you embrace the importance of this word, you are embarking on a new journey of self-discovery as you begin to easily chart a new course for yourself using one simple yet awesomely powerful word. Go ahead, try it on for size. Say it out loud!

When you think of it, we are all unbelievable, each one of us. We are unique in the eyes of God, made in His image with a purposeful life to lead. That's unbelievable all by itself, yet I refrain from digressing here. We're all God's people, and even though some can be quite unbelievable at times, there's goodness in everyone. Every unbelievable experience can also be a lesson if we're open and willing to see it.

Turn the page, keep reading, and start writing, designing, and living out more unbelievable stories— and I don't mean tall tales! As you go about your experiments with this magical word, try to notice the unbelievable kindness, compassion, and good-heartedness in everyone you meet.

Table of Contents

Part One

Magical Results

Chapter 1:

Words Matter—and *This One* Matters a Lot!

"Raise your words, not your voice.
It is rain that grows flowers, not thunder."
—Rumi

The impetus for writing this book now came from a recent client experience at my hypnotherapy practice.

Peter sought hypnosis as a tool for helping him improve his self-esteem and confidence. A very shy and socially anxious young man, he wanted to see some fast improvements while also wanting a long-term skill-building solution for life.

He shared a dilemma he was having when it came to speaking with others and wanted to lift his spirits, his hope, and ultimately his whole mindset. We did some hypnosis work, and he left with a posthypnotic suggestion to try something new.

He found himself getting a bit depressed and stuck in a rut with the same conversation at the desk when he checked into his gym. His rote response to "How are you doing?" was always "Good, and you?" It was the automatic response that people make as a matter of routine.

I asked Peter to change it up for a couple of weeks, as difficult as it may have seemed for such a shy guy. I asked him to experiment and change his response. Instead of the habitual "Good, and you?" response, he changed his response to "Unbelievable," delivered with a more confident voice. I had him practicing it in the mirror, smiling at himself, and just trying it on for size.

Over the course of two weeks, the results were astonishingly positive, and they can be for you as well, as you'll soon discover. Peter expanded his use of the word to other areas of his life. His family and friends noticed, and most importantly, he noticed it. Every time he used it with emphasis and positivity, he noticed a change taking place. He was actually programming his own mind for success, and he noticed the change in responses he received from others. Amazing, right? Unbelievable!

Peter's results are yours for the asking, simply by starting to build your own esteem and confidence, as well as your influence and persuasion skills.

So this book is written to hopefully move you toward greater influence and persuasion effectiveness in conversation with others and, more importantly, toward improving your own self-programming to see that new, more effective, happier, and more confident you begin to shine.

The English language is vast and filled with a seemingly infinite number of words. I suppose it's equally true for all spoken languages. And each one of those words has the power to evoke a certain feeling or emotion. Yet the spoken vocabulary of the majority is very limited.

So add the word *unbelievable* to your repertoire—today!

The word *unbelievable* can be used as an adjective or an adverb. When used as an adjective, it means that something is too good or impossible to be true. For example, "She got accepted into all eight Ivy League schools? That's unbelievable!" When used as an adverb, it means that something happened with great force or intensity. For example, "He hit the ball so unbelievably hard that it went clear out of the park. Unbelievable!"

Words matter for another reason as well. The spoken word, after it lands on our ear, travels deep inside our brain and causes thoughts, feelings, and actions. More later about that magical system, which we call the reticular activating system or RAS.

Definition

The *Merriam-Webster* dictionary defines "unbelievable" as "incredible." In other words, it's something that's so good or astounding that it's difficult to believe. The word *unbelievable* can also be used to describe something that's beyond the realm of comprehension. It's simply too amazing or astounding for us to understand. For example, "The way she handled that situation was unbelievable."

Synonyms

There are a number of words that have similar meanings to unbelievable. Some of these include incredible, amazing, phenomenal, mind-blowing, and jaw-dropping. Other synonyms for unbelievable include astounding, astonishing, implausible, incredible, outlandish, preposterous, marvelous, unimaginable, and unthinkable. Check your *Funk and Wagnalls* for a more complete list!

As you play with words, specifically with unbelievable, salt your conversation with a few synonyms and observe.

Here are a few examples showing how you can use unbelievable in a sentence:

- I can't believe that he ate the entire pizza by himself! That's incredibly unbelievable!

- I'm still in shock over winning the lottery. It feels amazingly unbelievable!
- The sun setting over the ocean is an unbelievable sight. Mind-blowing.
- She ran the marathon in under three hours? That's simply unbelievable!
- After years of being unemployed, he finally got a job offer. We were all unbelieving, but it's true!
- He drives an unbelievably fast car.
- They had an unbelievably large house.

As you can see from the examples above, the word *unbelievable* is quite versatile. It can be used to describe something that's too good to be true or something that happened with great force or intensity.

The power of a single word is often underestimated. Yet the right word can have a profound impact on our lives. Words matter in any communication because they convey our thoughts and feelings. They can persuade and influence others and create an unbelievable effect. Whether we are communicating with friends, family, or coworkers, the right word can make all the difference in the outcome of our communication effort.

Ivan Petrovich Pavlov, of "Pavlov's dog" fame and his conditioning experiments, was a renowned scientist focused on the conditioning of the human nervous system, primarily through work with dogs. He was also intrigued by hypnosis, sleep, and the impact that words have on the human condition. Pavlov's work with classical conditioning had a huge influence on how humans perceive themselves, their behavior, and their learning processes. His research on classical conditioning is still essential to contemporary behavior treatment.

Suffice it to say for our purposes here, Pavlov's research on the spoken word and its impact on human behavior is well established. I mention it here to shine a little bit of light on the science. It's a heavy read, but you can explore it more in the 1930 book, *The Word as a Physiological and Therapeutic Factor: The Theory and Practice of Psychotherapy According to I. P. Pavlov*, by K. I. Platanov.

> *"Men are apt to be much more influenced by words than by the actual facts of the surrounding reality."*
> —Ivan Pavlov

When it comes to having influential conversations, there is one word that has the power to make or break your message: *unbelievable.* This word has the ability to instantly change the tone of a conversation and can be the difference between sounding interested or bored.

For example, the word *unbelievable* is often used to describe something that is simply too good to be true. However, it can also be used to describe something that is so terrible it defies belief. In other words, the same word can have opposite meanings depending on how it's used. This word has the ability to influence our perception of reality. If someone tells us something we find hard to believe, we are more likely to believe it if they use the word *unbelievable*.

As you are aware, the way we communicate with people can be greatly impacted by the words we use. The wrong word can cause miscommunications, misunderstandings, and even conflict. The right word can influence, persuade, and even inspire others. Sometimes we hear a word incorrectly and respond incorrectly as well.

The ability to persuade people is a valuable skill. It can be used to convince people to see things your way, take action, or make a purchase. By understanding the psychology of persuasion, you can learn to use persuasive techniques in your own life. The word *unbelievable* is a powerful tool in anyone's persuasion arsenal.

Unbelievable Word Power

In 1962, during the Cuban Missile Crisis, President John F. Kennedy was briefing the press about the situation. When asked how close the U.S. was to war, Kennedy misheard the question and responded, "We're eyeball to eyeball." The press misinterpreted Kennedy's response as confirmation that the U.S. was, in fact, close to war when in reality, he meant that they were in a standoff and neither side wanted to back down. This misunderstanding could have led to an all-out nuclear war if not for Kennedy's quick thinking and ability to clarify his statement. I would say that Kennedy was unbelievably quick on his feet in a very serious situation.

The power of a single word is incredible. In just a few short syllables, we can communicate complex ideas and provoke strong emotions. We can make people laugh, cry, or even start a revolution. The right word at the right time can change the course of history.

Hypnotic Influence

Hypnotic influence involves the power of words to influence another person's thoughts, attitudes, or behaviors. It is a phenomenon that has been documented throughout history and into modern times. Hypnotic influence typically relies on a combination of verbal suggestion and heightened suggestibility, which can be enhanced with techniques such as visual imagery or rhythmic breathing.

In modern times, hypnotic influence is used to help people with a variety of issues. It can be used to help people overcome addictions, reduce anxiety, and even manage physical pain. Hypnosis has also been shown to be successful in helping people overcome phobias and other emotional issues.

Hypnotic influence has also been used in marketing to persuade people to make a purchase or change their behavior. It can be used in subtle ways, such as by suggesting a product is the best choice or more directly with techniques like repetitive phrases or eye fixation.

Hypnotic influence has also been used in politics to influence public opinion.

In 1975, Gerald Ford was running for president against Jimmy Carter. During a televised debate, as reported, Ford made an unbelievable mistake by stating that there was no Soviet domination of Eastern Europe. This statement gave Carter the opportunity to highlight Ford's lack of foreign policy experience and helped him win the election. A single word can also have a huge influence on people's opinions. In politics, the choice of words is often carefully calibrated to sway public opinion. A gaffe like Ford's can be costly, while a well-timed quip can make a candidate seem more relatable and likable.

While it's not clear what exactly caused Ford to make this gaffe, some experts believe that he may have been confused by the use of the word "dominate." The Soviets had a strong presence in many Eastern European countries, but they didn't actually control them. This mistake cost Ford the election and showed just how important words can be in politics.

11

Words matter. Our subconscious mind assigns meaning. The mind cannot really act on the word *unbelievable*, except to hone in and pay closer attention!

Undetected Persuasion

In 1858, Abraham Lincoln was running for senator from Illinois. His opponent, Stephen Douglas, was a popular incumbent senator and had been in office for many years. Douglas decided to attack Lincoln by accusing him of being two-faced and inconsistent on key issues. Lincoln's response was the famous "A house divided against itself cannot stand" speech, which helped him win the election and become one of America's most iconic presidents.

That was an unbelievable response by Lincoln!

The right words can be very persuasive. In Lincoln's case, he used a simple analogy to refute Douglas's charges and make a compelling argument for his own candidacy. A single word can make all the difference in a close race. While the power of a single word is great, it's important to use words carefully. Misunderstanding and conflict can often result from poor communication. The wrong word at the wrong time can have disastrous consequences. But when used correctly, words can be a powerful tool for good. They can influence people's opinions, persuade them to take action, and even change the course of history. Unbelievable, isn't it?

The word *unbelievable* is incredibly powerful because it has the ability to influence people's opinions and emotions. It can make people laugh, cry, or even start a revolution. The right word at the right time can change the course of history. *Unbelievable* is such a potent word because it's full of emotion and can be interpreted in many ways. It's a word that can make people believe in something, even if it isn't true.

- I can't believe you ate all of that cake! Unbelievable!
- The Challenger explosion was truly unbelievable.
- To this day, I still find it unbelievable that we won the lottery.
- After weeks of planning, her party's success was unbelievable.
- It's unbelievable that you would say something like that!
- I find it unbelievable that he would say something like that.
- I had an unbelievable hot air balloon flight.

By using *unbelievable* strategically, you can make your conversations more meaningful, improve relationships, and add a positive and uplifting tone to any discussion. Start using the word today and watch your personal brand grow!

Here are seven reasons why you should start using the word *unbelievable* in your conversations:

1. It shows that you're engaged in the conversation. People will notice that you're listening and paying attention when you use the word *unbelievable*. It makes people think about what you're saying in a different way. *Unbelievable* can help to make your point stand out from the crowd and be remembered for longer. It shows enthusiasm and excitement, which can be contagious and help to draw others into the conversation. It's a great way to show surprise or disbelief in a situation without over-exaggerating or coming across as too dramatic. It can add humor to your conversations, making them more enjoyable for everyone involved.

2. It conveys your interest in what the other person is saying. When you use the word, it shows that you are genuinely engaged in the discussion. It suggests that what's being discussed is worth excitedly talking about. It gives you a chance to provide feedback and share your thoughts on the matter.

3. It demonstrates that you're listening to and comprehending what's being said. You can use the word *unbelievable* to show that you're taking notice of what's being said and that you understand it. It shows your appreciation for something that has been done well. Showing your appreciation builds relationships, as people know their efforts have been recognized.

4. It gives you a chance to provide feedback and share your thoughts on the matter. A simple *unbelievable* can be a powerful way to express your feelings without appearing overly critical. It shows that you're open to new ideas and willing to learn from others. When you use the word *unbelievable*, it opens up a dialogue between you and other people who may have different perspectives. People are more likely to stay engaged in a conversation.

5. It allows you to build rapport with the other person by showing them that you have similar interests. It allows you to be memorable and stand out in a crowd. The word has an uplifting connotation, which can make conversations more positive and help keep the conversation going. It encourages creative thinking, as people will often think of interesting examples when hearing the word *unbelievable*. It can be used to highlight moments of success and accomplishment, helping you build a strong relationship with the other person. When something truly extraordinary has been achieved, saying, "That's unbelievable," is an effective way to show your admiration for the achievement.

6. It gives you an opportunity to bond with the other person over a shared experience. When you both talk about the unbelievable thing that happened or was said, it gives you something to connect over and makes your conversation even more special. It helps build a sense of trust with the other person. When you use the word

unbelievable in conversations, it implies a certain openness and willingness to believe the story that the other person is telling. It allows you to express a sense of awe and admiration for something. When something truly amazing happens, it can be hard to put into words just how great it was. But using the word *unbelievable* conveys exactly how much you appreciate what happened or what was said. It's a great way to show your appreciation and enthusiasm for the moment.

7. It shows that you are open-minded and willing to consider new ideas. Lastly, it allows you to show humility and gratitude in a way that is sincere. Using the word *unbelievable* when expressing appreciation for something can be an incredibly powerful gesture, as it shows that you're genuinely grateful for what was done.

By incorporating the word *unbelievable* into your conversations, you can demonstrate an openness to new ideas, creativity and growth, confidence in persuasion, empathy and understanding, and a strong personal brand. When you use it in your own self-talk with positive intentions, it boosts your state and shifts your whole mindset.

Saying *unbelievable*, you will instantly sound more engaged, interested, and influential in any conversation. It demonstrates that you are confident. People often have a positive response to those who express confidence in their opinions by using the word *unbelievable.* This can help you gain respect and establish trust with your audience. Isn't that the goal?

When you use the word *unbelievable,* you are expressing admiration and appreciation for the ideas of someone else. This shows that you value their opinion, which in turn strengthens your relationship with them. Keep in mind that it also demonstrates sincere empathy and understanding. Unbelievable is a word that can be used to express amazement and admiration for someone else's success or accomplishments. This helps build bridges of understanding between you and your peers and establishes mutual respect.

There's something magical about the sound of the word falling on one's ears. Perhaps it activates that system deep in our mind that wakes us from a trance and causes us to pause and focus, as if our subconscious mind is saying, "Hey, pay close attention to what comes next. It sounds like it could be important."

Chapter 2:

Stoics and Poker Faces

First learn the meaning of what you say,
and then speak.
—Epictetus, Stoic philosopher

Stoics make an art of choosing words carefully and with a very controlled, straight face.

As the *Daily Stoic* explains (at dailystoic.com):

"The ancient Stoic philosophers came from almost every imaginable background. One was a slave; another was an emperor. One was a water carrier, another a famous playwright. Some were merchants, others were independently wealthy. Some were Senators and others were soldiers. What they all had in common was the philosophy that they practiced. Whether they were chafing under the shackles of slavery or leading the Roman army, they focused not on the external world but on what was solely in their own control: Their own thoughts, their own actions, their beliefs. Below are some short biographies of some of the most influential stoics, including Marcus Aurelius, Seneca, Epictetus, Cato, Zeno, Cleanthes, Hecato, Musonius Rufus. It's important to remember that these are only the Stoics whose names survive to us—for every one of them there are dozens or hundreds of other brilliant, brave minds, whose legacy is lost to us."

Why the Word *Unbelievable* is So Powerful

In any given conversation, there are a few key words that can instantly change the entire dynamic. One of those words is *unbelievable*. This word has the power to instantly influence the direction of any conversation— for better or for worse.

Let's take a look at how the word *unbelievable* can be used in conversations, and we'll also look at some of the top reasons for adding it to your vocabulary.

The Stoics Knew the Power of *Unbelievable*

The Stoics were essentially a collective school of thought that flourished in ancient Greece and Rome. Stoicism is founded on the belief that negative emotions are caused by our own thoughts and perceptions and that by changing them, we can achieve inner peace. Many of the most famous Stoics were philosophers, such as

Epictetus, Seneca, and Marcus Aurelius. The Stoics understood the power of *unbelievable* and used it to their advantage. In their philosophy, they taught that by maintaining composure in the face of adversity, one could maintain control over their emotions and avoid being swayed by outside influences. In other words, they knew that emotional self-control was key to creating confidence and charisma—two things that are essential for success in any business conversation.

In their writings, these philosophers often used the word *unbelievable* to describe their own philosophy. For example, Marcus Aurelius wrote, "It is unbelievable how much may be done if one takes care not to become ensnared in public affairs."

Epictetus said, "It is unbelievable how little trouble there actually is in life if one just sets his mind not to give it any."

And Seneca wrote, "It is unbelievable how soon things change from good to bad..."

These quotes show us how Stoics use the word *unbelievable* to describe their own philosophy. They use it to emphasize how simple it can be to achieve inner peace if we just change our thoughts and perceptions.

Further examples of Stoic use of the word: Epictetus would say that it is unbelievable that we are alive. Seneca was known to say that it is unbelievable that we have a soul. Marcus Aurelius supposedly said that it is unbelievable that we are human beings. Each of these Stoics used the word *unbelievable* in a different way to explain their own philosophy.

There are many reasons why you should add *unbelievable* to your vocabulary. Not only is it a great attention grabber and very versatile, but it also shows inner confidence, creates an air of mystery and curiosity, and demonstrates fabulous emotional self-control. Think about it for a moment. When you hear someone speak calmly, their words have power, don't they?

When you're looking for a way to inject some excitement into a conversation or create an impactful impression, consider using this power word—you may be surprised at just how influential it can be!

Now that we know why *unbelievable* is such a powerful word from a linguistic perspective. Let's focus briefly on how we can use it to our advantage in business. Here are a few examples:

"That offer is unbelievable!"

"I can't believe how much progress we've made!"

"I'm sorry, but I find that hard to believe."

"That's an unbelievable story!"

"I don't believe what I'm hearing."

"Sales are unbelievable."

I am certain you are already experimenting with this newly reactivated word in your vocabulary—at least I hope so! Let's continue.

7 Stoic Reasons for Adding *Unbelievable* to Your Vocabulary

1. It's a strong word that packs a punch.

Unbelievable is a very strong word that can really pack a punch when used correctly. For example, if you're in a meeting and want to make a strong impression, you could say, "That offer is unbelievable!" and everyone will be sure to take notice.

2. It's a great way to emphasize a point.

Another great use of *unbelievable* is to emphasize a point you're making. For example, if you want to show how successful you've been, you could say, "I can't believe how much progress we've made!" and your listeners will be impressed by your accomplishments.

3. It's a great attention grabber.

If you want to draw someone's attention to what you're saying, using the word *unbelievable* is a great way to do it. For example, if you're telling an exciting story, you could say, "This an unbelievable story!" and your listener will be glued to your every word.

4. It shows confidence.

In virtually any conversation, when you use the word *unbelievable*, it shows that you have confidence in what you're saying. This can be very appealing to others and can make them more likely to trust what you have to say. People will trust you more when they see that you believe in yourself.

5. It sets you apart from others.

The word *unbelievable* is not one that everyone uses, so using it can help set you apart from the competition and differentiate you from others. When people hear this word, they'll know that you're not like other people and that you have something unique to offer. It shows that you are an independent thinker.

6. It shows you're in control of your emotions.

The Stoics believed that one of the keys to inner peace was emotional self-control. When you use the word *unbelievable*, it shows that you're in control of your emotions and that nothing can shake your composure.

7. It creates an emotional reaction in others.

The last reason why the word *unbelievable* is so powerful is because it creates an emotional reaction in others. For example, if someone doesn't believe what they're hearing, they might get upset or angry. This shows that the word has the ability to influence people's emotions, which can be very powerful indeed.

Emotional Self-Control and Calmness Create Confidence and Charisma

Are you ready to mold that magnetic personality?

Let's consider your choice to tune up your vocabulary as a major deliberate step in shaping your very destiny in life. Yes, it's that powerful because new doors, new opportunities, and new challenges lie ahead, and new levels of happiness are in your crosshairs. Keep vigilant.

The word *unbelievable* creates an air of mystery in any conversation: It can arouse curiosity around you, which can make you more intriguing and interesting to others, and it shows emotional self-control because it requires you to refrain from showing any emotion in your voice or on your face (i.e.., you must maintain a poker face). This demonstrates discipline and restraint, which are both qualities that are highly prized in business circles as well as in general conversation.

Overall, the word *unbelievable* is a powerful tool that can be used in many different ways. Whether you're trying to grab someone's attention or emphasize a point, *unbelievable* can help you do that. In addition, using *unbelievable* can also show others that you're confident and in control of your emotions—both of which are important ingredients for creating charisma and influence. At the risk of being a bit redundant, it's a powerful word because it has the ability to stop people in their tracks. It's a word that instantly grabs people's attention and causes them to sit up and take notice.

When you use *unbelievable*, you are immediately injecting a high level of interest and excitement into the conversation. How might you use the word *unbelievable* in discussing these quotes?

> "People are disturbed, not by things, but by the views they take of them." —Epictetus

> "Most people are upset not by what happens to them, but by their opinion of what happens to them." —Seneca

> "It is not death that a man should fear, but he should fear never beginning to live." —Marcus Aurelius

As you play with the word usage, be aware of your inner dialogue too. Practice this for a few days when you awaken. Say something like this as soon as your feet touch the ground, preferably earlier:

> "Every day and in every way, I am better and better. In fact, I feel more unbelievable with each passing day as I grow into the person I am; brave, courageous, and strong, taking bold steps and living the purpose of my life as my Creator leads me."

You can use lots of variations. You'll build your own self-programming affirmations as you go.

Chapter 3:

Salespeople Know This Secret

*"Repeat anything often enough and
it will start to become you."*
—Tom Hopkins

Let's take Mr. Hopkins literally here.

Repeat the word *unbelievable* in your inner and outer conversations, and it will indeed start to become you! I suggest a positive outlook, however, to keep you moving forward!

In sales, words are powerful. The ability to use words strategically can be the difference between closing a deal and walking away empty-handed. That's why world-renowned sales trainer Tom Hopkins advises salespeople to say *unbelievable* when trying to close a deal. Here's why:

How to Use the Word *Unbelievable* in Sales to Close More Deals

The vocabulary that salespeople use can have a significant impact on whether or not they close a deal. For example, consider the word *unbelievable*. When used correctly, this word can convey excitement and urgency, two emotions that are critical in closing a sale.

Think about it—if a prospective customer is on the fence about buying your product or service, hearing that it's *unbelievable* might just be the push they need to make a decision. After all, who doesn't want to be seen as someone who makes *unbelievable* decisions?

Ever wonder why so many salespeople use the word *unbelievable* when trying to close a deal? It's not just because they're trying to be dramatic; it's actually a technique that can be traced back to legendary sales trainer Tom Hopkins. In this blog post, we'll explore why Hopkins recommends using this particular word and how you can use it to your advantage when trying to close more sales.

Tom Hopkins is considered one of the foremost authorities on selling, and for good reason. He's been training salespeople for over forty years and has helped countless individuals close more deals and increase their earnings. One of the key pieces of advice he gives his students is to use the word *unbelievable* strategically in conversation.

According to Hopkins, *unbelievable* has three key benefits when used correctly. First, it shows that you're confident in what you're selling. Second, it helps build rapport with the person you're speaking to by showing that you're on their side (i.e., you understand that what you're asking them to believe is, in fact, unbelievable). And third, it creates a sense of urgency by implying that if they don't act now, they may miss out on a once-in-a-lifetime opportunity. He also recommends using it early on in the conversation so as not to give your prospect the impression that you're desperate to make a sale. Finally, he recommends being specific about why you believe your product or service is unbelievable so as not to come across as disingenuous.

Of course, as with anything in sales (or life), there's a fine line between using *unbelievable* effectively and coming off as desperate or insincere. The key is to use it sparingly and only when you truly believe in what you're selling. If you overuse it or use it in situations where it doesn't make sense, you'll only end up hurting your chances of closing the deal.

Of course, while the word *unbelievable* can be powerful, as I just mentioned above, it's important to use it sparingly. If every other word out of your mouth is *unbelievable*, it will quickly become meaningless. Hopkins advises salespeople to use the word only when they truly believe that what they're saying is incredible. When used in this way, the word can be an effective tool for closing deals.

A wise salesperson will utilize the word strategically and also listen intently for a client or prospect to use the word in business conversation. For example:

- "It's unbelievable how much money I've saved by switching to your company's services."
- "It's unbelievable how much easier my life has become since I started using your product."
- "The results I got from using your product were simply unbelievable."
- "When I saw the price, I couldn't believe it was so low."

By following Hopkins' advice, you can make sure you're using the word *unbelievable* in a way that is both effective and believable.

So, in wrapping up this chapter, let me underscore the importance of using the right words in selling. In today's competitive marketplace, it's important for salespeople to use every tool at their disposal to close deals. One often overlooked tool is the power of words. By strategically using words like *unbelievable*, salespeople can create excitement and urgency, both of which are critical in getting prospective customers to say "Yes." So, the next time you're trying to close a deal, don't forget the power of Tom Hopkins' advice—and don't be afraid to use the word *unbelievable*. It just might be the key to unlocking success.

Chapter 4:

Instant Hypnotic Induction and Fast Hypnotic Influence

Isn't it unbelievable how magical words can seem to be? Imagine how you might begin to use the word *unbelievable* in conversation with ethical influence and persuasion as your intent. If you want to get someone's attention quickly and easily, there's no better word to use than *unbelievable*. It's a powerful, attention-grabbing word that can instantly hypnotize someone and make them more open to influence.

I use *unbelievable* daily in client conversations at my hypnotherapy practice. While this book is not intended to formally introduce you to the field of hypnosis, this chapter gives you enough insight to effectively use the word *unbelievable* or other high-impact, attention-getting words in strategic conversations.

Here's how it works:

When you use the word *unbelievable*, you are effectively bypassing the conscious mind and going straight for the subconscious. The subconscious mind is much more open to suggestion and influence than the conscious mind, so by using this word, you can quickly get someone into a suggestible state.

In order to make the most of this technique, it's important to use it in a way that's congruent with the message you want to communicate. For example, if you're trying to sell someone on a new product, you could say something like, "This product is so unbelievable, I can't even begin to describe it!"

If you're trying to get someone to do something for you, you could say, "I would be unbelievably grateful if you could do this for me." You can compound the positive effect of such a statement by adding another magic word: *because*. For example, if you were to say, "Because this is so important... I would be unbelievably grateful if you could do this for me," you increase your ability to achieve compliance. Consider these examples:

1. I would be unbelievably grateful if you could pick up my dry cleaning for me.

2. Because this is so important, I would be unbelievably grateful if you could help me study for my test this afternoon.

3. Because you deserve to enjoy the very best, let me just say that I can't believe how unbelievable this product is, it's definitely worth buying!

The key is to use the word in a way that feels natural and genuine. If you try to force it, it will come across as disingenuous, and people will see right through it. Be careful but be brave and try it! You are creating hypnotic influence and offering up suggestions to the listener's subconscious mind. This technique of identifying precise language patterns is known as neuro-linguistic programming or NLP. It's a powerful tool that can be used to influence and persuade people in a variety of ways. If you're not familiar with NLP, which is far beyond the scope of this book, I highly recommend checking it out. There are many good programs on NLP. I recommend starting with *Excellence in NLP and Coaching* by Dr. Richard Nongard.

Let's get back to the subject at hand. I want to introduce you to hypnosis so that you have enough background information to know how powerful words such as *unbelievable* can be in any conversation. When you use *unbelievable* in conversation, applied gingerly and strategically, you're creating an instant hypnotic induction that, in many cases, stops people in their tracks momentarily, creating an opportunity for suggestion or hypnotic influence.

I mentioned that I use the word *unbelievable* in client conversations in my office. I might say something like this to a client, to share one example:

"As you take your next relaxing breath and pause for a moment... you might begin to notice your whole body... and your mind starting to enjoy an unbelievable feeling of comfort... and you might even begin to realize that you do, indeed, have the power to take back control of things... how you respond to others, how your awareness increases quite... well... unbelievably or so it seems."

What is Hypnosis?

Hypnosis is an altered state of consciousness in which a person is more open to suggestion and influence. In a hypnotic state, also known as a resource state, a person's conscious mind is bypassed, and the subconscious mind is more open to suggestion. Essentially, resistance is lowered, and the mind is more open to entertaining new ideas and perspectives. This can be used to achieve various goals, such as changing a behavior or increasing motivation.

Hypnosis can be induced in a variety of ways, but the most common is through verbal suggestion. This is why it's so important to be strategic with your words when you're trying to influence someone. The right words, spoken in the right way, can have a profound effect on the listener. There are different types of hypnotic inductions, but the one I want to focus on here is known as an "instant induction." This is a type of hypnosis that can be induced very quickly, often in just a few seconds. It's based on the power of suggestion and works by taking advantage of a person's natural tendency to follow along with what they're hearing.

The Purpose of Hypnotic Inductions

Hypnotic inductions occur naturally throughout the day as attention shifts and people change their focus and concentration. They also occur with the aid of a hypnotist or by using self-hypnosis to prepare the mind for hearing both direct and indirect suggestions. The purpose of hypnotic induction is to shift the focus of attention away from the conscious mind and into the subconscious mind. This allows for suggestions to be made that can influence the person's thoughts, emotions, and behavior. The induction can be quick or even instant, or it can be a gradual process that uses relaxation, imagery, and visualization to help the subconscious mind dissociate from the conscious mind, allowing or preparing the mind to hear and embrace suggestions in alignment with intention.

Seven Tips for Creating a Rapid Hypnotic Induction

1. Use believable words.

When you use believable words in a conversation, you are creating an instant hypnotic induction. This is because people are more likely to follow along with what they're hearing when the words sound believable. The right words spoken in the right way can have a profound effect on the listener. So it's no coincidence that the word *unbelievable* is so powerful!

2. Be strategic with your intonation.

Your tone of voice is just as important as the words you use when you're trying to hypnotize someone. This is because the way you say something can be just as influential as the words you use. For example, if you were to say the word *unbelievable* with a rising intonation, it would sound more like a question than a statement. This would make it much less likely to induce hypnosis. However, if you said the word *unbelievable* with a falling intonation, it would sound more like a statement of fact. This would be much more likely to induce hypnosis.

3. Use rhythms and patterns.

People are more likely to follow along with what they're hearing when it's presented in a rhythmic or patterned way. This is because our brains are wired to recognize and respond to patterns. So when you use rhythms and patterns in your speech, you're effectively creating a hypnotic induction. Be congruent with your intentions, and the right words will follow. Your words, tone of voice, and body language should all be in alignment if you want to create a powerful hypnotic induction. This is because people are more likely to follow along with what they're hearing when the message is consistent. So if you want to induce hypnosis using the word *unbelievable*, make sure that your words, tone of voice, and body language are all conveying the same message.

4. Be clear and concise.

When you're giving a suggestion, be clear and concise with your language. Don't try to overload the person with too much information at once. Stick to the main point and keep your language simple and easy to understand.

5. Use positive language. Be specific.

Use positive language when giving suggestions. This will help increase the likelihood of success in your communications. Negative language can often be met with resistance by the listener, so it's best to avoid it whenever possible. The more specific you are with your suggestions, the more likely they are to be successful. This is because people are more likely to follow along with what they're hearing when it's presented in a clear and concise way. So if you want to use the word *unbelievable* to induce hypnosis, make sure that your suggestion is specific. For example, rather than saying, "You will feel more relaxed," say, "You will feel your muscles relax and your mind calm."

6. Be mindful of tonality and pacing.

Be mindful of your tonality and pacing when delivering suggestions. Try to speak slowly and clearly, and make sure to maintain a consistent tone throughout your conversation. Pacing is also important, so make sure to adjust your speaking speed accordingly depending on the person you're speaking to.

7. Be aware of body language cues.

Be aware of the body language cues of the person you're speaking to in order to gauge their level of receptiveness and how open they are to your suggestions.

Finally, as a bonus, make it easy for the person to say "Yes" to your request, whatever it may be. When you're making a suggestion, make it easy for the person to say "Yes" by using language that's in alignment with their current reality. For example, if you want to suggest that the person relax, you might say, "You are already feeling more relaxed." This is because it's easier for the person to agree with a suggestion that's in alignment with their current reality. If you use language that is not in alignment with the person's current reality, they're likely to resist the suggestion.

The Power of Suggestion: How to Use Words Strategically to Influence People

1. The word *unbelievable* is very influential because it has the ability to capture attention and induce

hypnosis. For example, you might say, "This is unbelievable," to get someone's attention.

2. The word *yes* is very influential because it's easy for people to say, and it reinforces the suggestion. For example, you might say, "Yes, that sounds good," to agree with someone's suggestion.

3. The word *now* is very influential because it creates a sense of urgency and encourages the person to act immediately. For example, you might say, "Now is the time to take action," to encourage someone to act quickly.

4. The word *easy* is very influential because it makes the suggestion seem less daunting and more achievable. For example, you might say, "It's easy to relax your mind and body," to suggest that relaxation is easy to achieve.

5. The word *you* is very influential because it puts the focus on the person and makes them feel important. For example, you might say, "You are in control of your own destiny," to empower someone.

6. The word *will* is very influential because it implies that the outcome is certain. For example, you might say, "You will succeed," in order to increase the chances of success.

7. The word *change* is very influential because it suggests that something will be different after taking action. For example, you might say, "A change for the

better is possible," in order to inspire someone to take action.

Now, review the above examples of these seven powerful words and combine them to make an influential statement. You can do it!

Chapter 5:

The Unbelievable Power of Suggestion: Murphy's Insights

"The only limit to our realization of tomorrow will be our doubts of today."
—Franklin D. Roosevelt

It's hard to believe that something as simple as suggestion could have such a profound impact on our behavior, but that's exactly what renowned author and lecturer Joseph Murphy asserts in his book, *The Power of Your Subconscious Mind,* and other equally insightful books. According to Murphy, the human mind is incredibly suggestible and can be easily influenced by the thoughts and suggestions of others. In fact, he believes that our belief system—or the set of beliefs we hold about ourselves—is largely determined by the suggestions we receive from others throughout our lives. (I can attest to this as a professional hypnotist!)

Murphy cites the work of French psychologist Émile Coué, who popularized the concept of autosuggestion or self-suggestion in the early twentieth century. Coué believed that we have the power to change our lives for the better by making positive suggestions to ourselves *on a regular basis.* Murphy agrees with this notion and provides numerous examples throughout the book of how autosuggestion has helped people overcome various challenges in their lives.

1. Murphy recounts the story of a woman who was able to overcome her fear of public speaking through the use of autosuggestion.

2. He also tells the story of a man who was able to overcome his fear of flying by using self-hypnosis.

3. And he describes how a woman was able to get over her fear of water through the power of positive thinking.

4. In each of these cases, and many others, Murphy shows how the power of suggestion can help us overcome our fears and achieve our goals.

The bottom line is that our thoughts and beliefs have a direct impact on our behavior. If we believe we can't do something, chances are we won't even try. But if we believe we can, we're much more likely to succeed. As I said in the introduction to this book, *When I see it, I'll believe it* may be widely remembered, but *When I believe it, I'll see it* is a far more powerful twist on the phrase.

Murphy also recounts the case of a woman who used autosuggestion to lose weight and keep it off. He writes about a guy who overcame his arachnophobia with the help of autosuggestion. Finally, Murphy discusses the situation of a woman who used autosuggestion to repair her marital difficulties. I wonder what changes or shifts in their belief system helped to make the changes they sought. I wonder if you are using power words such as *unbelievable* to see and feel different.

You may be familiar with Émile Coué's famous phrase: "Every day, in every way, I am getting better and better." This means that every day we can get a little bit better, and over time, we will get better and better. People have used this phrase to help them overcome their fears, lose weight, and fix their relationships. The idea is that if we keep telling ourselves we will get better, we eventually will. By setting a positive expectancy we are programming ourselves to move in the direction of true progress toward the realization of our intention.

The golfer could use the phrase "Every day, in every way, I am getting better and better" to help her improve her golf game. By repeating this phrase to herself on a regular basis, she will eventually start to see improvements in her skills. The more she believes it, the more likely it is to happen.

The same goes for you: If you want to improve your life in some way, make a positive suggestion to yourself on a regular basis, and eventually, you will start to see results. Just remember, the power of suggestion is an incredibly powerful tool that can help you achieve your goals.

The very purpose of using self-hypnosis is to feed our mind positive suggestions that are aligned with our intentions, and when those intentions are matched by a change in behaviors, the subconscious mind will more readily adopt and apply those that best fit. So autosuggestion could be far more than simply repeating an affirmation such as "I am getting better and better." To make it more believable and influential, we might want to say something like, "I used to struggle with my golf game, but now I see improvement every day I play. My swing is getting smoother, and my scores are getting lower. As I relax and enjoy the game more, my confidence is rising, and I allow my mind and body to bring a consistently good performance to each shot I take."

Now, add the word *unbelievable* to your statement:

"I am going to have an unbelievable outing on the course today. My mind is clear. I am relaxed, calm, and in complete control of my emotions. I already feel unbelievable because I know that I can do this. I visualize and mentally rehearse, and I step into my circle of excellence."

Or:

"I have an unbelievable amount of energy today and feel great about myself. I'm going to use it to go for a run, work on that project I've been putting off, and then relax and enjoy my evening."

Play with the combination of words, thoughts, images, and feelings that help you bring your best self to the situation; be it on the links, in the business world, or at home with family and friends.

One of the earliest books on self-suggestion and autosuggestion was *Autoconditioning* by Hornell Hart, PhD. In it, he discusses the unbelievable power of suggestion and how to use it to achieve success in any area of life. Hart outlines a simple three-step process for using autosuggestion:

1) Choose a goal,
2) Come up with a statement that supports the goal, and
3) Repeat the statement regularly.

For example, if you want to lose weight, you could come up with a statement like "I am losing weight every day" or "It's unbelievable. With the little changes I am making, I notice that I am getting thinner and thinner." Repeating this statement regularly will help program your mind for success. It becomes a self-fulfilling prophecy.

Another example would be if you want to get better grades in school. You could come up with a statement like "I am doing well in school" or "I am a good student." Repeating this statement regularly will help increase your chances of success.

The key is to make the statement believable and positive. The more you believe it, the more likely it is to happen. So choose a goal, come up with a statement that supports it, and start repeating it regularly! Be aware, too, of the greater intention, the real reasons the goal achievement is so important. Losing weight may lead to better health and more energy. Doing well in school may help you get into the college of your dreams. Stating the positive outcome rather than just the action will add power to your autosuggestion.

Some people are naturally skeptical of the power of suggestion, but there is plenty of scientific evidence to support its efficacy. In one study, participants who were instructed to smile more during the day reported feeling happier than those who were not given the same instruction. Another study found that people who repeated positive affirmations had increased self-esteem and decreased anxiety.

A detailed discussion of affirmations is beyond the scope of this book, yet it's important to understand how they work. Joseph Murphy, in his book *The Power of Your Subconscious Mind*, provides some helpful insights.

First, he explains that we have two minds—the conscious mind and the subconscious mind. The conscious mind is the analytical, rational part of our brain that is responsible for our everyday thoughts and actions. The subconscious mind, on the other hand, is the part of our brain that controls our habits, emotions, and beliefs.

Murphy goes on to say that the subconscious mind is very powerful and can be influenced by positive or negative suggestions. He gives the example of a woman who is afraid of snakes. Every time she sees a snake, her heart rate increases, she feels anxious, and she breaks out in a cold sweat. These are all physical reactions that are controlled by the subconscious mind.

If, however, she was to repeatedly tell herself, "I am not afraid of snakes" or "Snakes are harmless," her subconscious mind would eventually believe these statements, and her physical reactions would change accordingly. She would no longer feel anxious or have a fear of snakes.

The same is true for affirmations. Repeating positive statements about oneself can change the way the subconscious mind thinks and feels. Over time, these changes will manifest in the physical world as well.

While some may be skeptical of the power of suggestion, there's no denying that it can have a major impact on our thoughts, emotions, and behavior. If you're open to the idea of using autosuggestion to improve your life, I highly recommend reading *The Power of Your Subconscious Mind* by Joseph Murphy. It's an enlightening and inspiring book that just might change the way you think about yourself and the world around you.

Let me suggest a few powerful affirmations here, which might be just what you need to start applying this auto-conditioning concept to your daily life. The beauty of adding the word *unbelievable* to an affirmation is that it makes it one hundred percent true!

1. "I am feeling unbelievably powerful and confident today."
2. "I can do anything I set my mind to, as I have always done."
3. "I am an unbelievable success."
4. "Everything I do is unbelievable."
5. "I am the most unbelievable person in the world."
6. "My power is unbelievable."
7. "My success is unbelievable."
8. "I am absolutely unbelievable!"

Let me add: "I attract success and abundance into my life. Today will be an unbelievable day!"

As you can see, these affirmations are short, simple, and to the point. They are also easy to remember and repeat throughout the day. I suggest saying them out loud in front of a mirror, if possible, at least once a day.

Start repeating these affirmations to yourself on a daily basis and see how your life changes for the better! You might also want to write them down and carry them with you so that you can read them whenever you have a few free moments.

You've made the first step toward positive change in your life just by reading this book. Now it's time to put theory into action and start using autosuggestion to enhance your health, wealth, and relationships! Remember that the power of suggestion is a very powerful instrument; use it wisely for the benefit of yourself and others.

Close your eyes for just a moment. Take a deep relaxing breath or two. Now...

Say, "Unbelievable days await me. I feel unbelievably confident in my ability to take more charge of my life!"

Now... smile and turn the page, please.

Chapter 6:

The Power of Self-Talk: Speak Better to and about Yourself

If one magical word like unbelievable can have such a powerful effect on our disposition, imagine making changes in your whole self-talk habitual regimen.

Most of us are completely unaware of the things we say to ourselves on a daily basis. However, the words we use to define ourselves have a hugely impactful influence over our lives and our destiny. In fact, self-talk is one of the most powerful tools we have at our disposal when it comes to creating the life, we want for ourselves. Self-talk is the inner dialogue that we have with ourselves on a constant basis. It's the voice in our head that offers commentary and guidance on everything we do. Depending on the language we choose, our self-talk can be either positive or negative. The words we use to define ourselves have a powerful impact on our lives, for better or for worse.

The words we use to describe ourselves have a direct impact on our self-image, which in turn affects our behavior and the choices we make in life. If we constantly tell ourselves that we're not good enough and that we'll never amount to anything, then it's no wonder we end up living lives of frustration and mediocrity. On the other hand, if we fill our heads with positive, empowering self-talk, then we open up a world of possibility and potential.

The Seven Pillars of Self

This is a good place to bring up a very important subject that is far outside the scope of this book yet completely relevant to your self-talk improvements! I'm talking about what I refer to as the seven foundational pillars of self:

- Self-care
- Self-respect
- Self-compassion
- Self-awareness
- Self-confidence
- Self-worthiness
- Self-love

The seven pillars of self are essential for anyone looking to improve their self-talk. These seven points provide a basic foundation for understanding and improving our relationship with ourselves. The first three points—self-care, self-respect, and self-compassion—focus on the importance of taking care of ourselves both physically and emotionally. The next three points—self-awareness, self-confidence, and self-worthiness—deal with our ability to understand and accept ourselves as we are. Finally, the last point—self-love—reminds us that we need to love and accept ourselves unconditionally.

We won't delve into them here, but I bring them to your attention, for as you adopt better self-talk language, you will accelerate your progress on this journey with a better awareness of these points and how you can more easily move forward in life. Each point deserves your undivided attention. Understanding the obstacles, your current self-talk in these seven areas, and deciding that you are worthy of your own (and God's) love will awaken a new, unstoppable you!

Each of these seven points are important in their own right, but they also work together to create a strong foundation for healthy self-talk. You can communicate more effectively to yourself by making progress in any one of these areas, which will help you become more conscious of your thoughts and feelings.

Self-Hypnosis and the Seven Pillars of Self

Self-hypnosis can be a powerful tool for helping to identify and address any potential changes within each of the seven pillars of self. By using self-hypnosis, we can access our subconscious mind, which is where our deepest thoughts and feelings reside. This can be a valuable tool for helping us to become more aware of the thoughts and emotions that drive our behavior.

Self-hypnosis can also be helpful in addressing any negative self-talk that we may have. If we are able to identify the thoughts and emotions that are causing us problems, we can then work on replacing them with more positive, empowering thoughts. This can be a powerful way to improve our self-talk and our self-image. For instance, in terms of self-compassion, I advise you to be bold and courageous enough to get to know yourself better in order to begin improving your dialogue:

1. Find a quiet place where you can relax and focus on your breath.
2. Visualize a safe and comfortable place where you can go whenever you need support and comfort.
3. Spend time each day focusing on self-compassionate thoughts and feelings, allowing yourself to feel the love and support that are available to you.

One simple but incredibly effective way to improve our self-talk is to use the word *unbelievable* when describing ourselves or our accomplishments. Why? Because when we say something is unbelievable, we are, in essence, telling ourselves that we're beyond what's considered normal or average. We're setting ourselves apart from the crowd and declaring that we're capable of greatness.

You and I already know that you are great, just as you are. You are enough! Yet we can always strive for better self-talk! Here are three quick examples of how you can use the word *unbelievable* to improve your self-talk:

1. "I am unbelievably talented."
2. "I am unbelievably successful."
3. "I am unbelievably beautiful/handsome."

By repeatedly declaring these things to ourselves, using positive and present tense language, we plant the seeds of belief in our minds, which will eventually grow into reality. So start (or continue!) using the word *unbelievable* today and watch your life transform before your very eyes. Take it all a step further and teach someone else how to start improving their own self-talk!

In addition to using the word *unbelievable* to improve our self-talk, there are a number of other things we can do to make sure our internal dialogue is working for us and not against us. Here are seven keys to improving our self-talk:

1. Being aware of the things you say to yourself is the first step in making sure your self-talk is positive and empowering. If you are constantly berating yourself or putting yourself down, then you need to become more mindful of the words you are using. Make a conscious effort to replace negative self-talk with positive affirmations, and watch your self-image and confidence improve dramatically. For example, instead of saying,

"I'm such a loser," try saying, "I am a confident and successful person."

The words we use to define ourselves have a direct impact on our behavior. If you want to change your behavior, then you need to start by changing the way you talk to and about yourself. Start using positive, uplifting language, and watch your life change for the better. Be careful of the words you use to define yourself, as they can become self-fulfilling prophecies. If you tell yourself that you're not good enough or that you'll never amount to anything, then it's likely that you'll end up living a life that reflects those beliefs. On the other hand, if you fill your head with positive, empowering self-talk, then you open up a world of possibility and potential.

2. Positive self-talk is essential for building self-confidence and achieving success. When you talk positively about yourself, you're telling your subconscious mind that you believe in your abilities and that you're capable of anything. This type of positive reinforcement will help motivate you to take action and reach your goals. Examine your journey through this book and see what new thoughts and actions emerge as a result of your focus. I wonder how aware you are of that new you that's emerging, one day at a time. One thought and new positive action at a time.

Change the way you talk about yourself in relation to others. Instead of saying, "I'm not as good as so-and-so," try saying, "I'm just as good as anyone else." By changing the way you compare yourself to others, you'll start to see yourself in a more positive light. Be careful of the words you use to describe your past experiences. If you find yourself constantly dwelling on negative experiences from your past, then it's time to start reframing those experiences in a more positive light. For example, instead of saying, "I failed that test," try saying, "I learned a lot from that experience." By changing the way you talk about your past experiences, you'll start to see them as learning opportunities instead of failures.

3. Use affirmative statements such as "I am," "I can," and "I will" when talking to yourself. These statements will help program your mind for success and inspire you to take massive action. Try adding this: Take a few comforting breaths and tell yourself that you can do anything you put your mind to, and you are simply unbelievably in more control than you probably ever imagined. Make sure your self-talk is specific, realistic, and measurable. For example, telling yourself, "I am going to be a millionaire," is much more effective than simply saying, "I want to be rich." The more specific and realistic your self-talk is, the easier it will be for you to take action and achieve your goals.

4. Avoid using negative words such as "can't," "won't," and "don't." These words will only serve to discourage and demoralize you, leading to a lack of motivation and decreased self-confidence. Pay close attention to the tone of your self-talk. If you find that you're constantly using negative critical language when you talk to yourself, then it's time to make a change. Instead, focus on using a positive, upbeat tone. For example, instead of saying, "I can't believe I'm such a screw-up," try saying, "I'm doing my best, and I know I can improve."

5. Use the present tense when talking to yourself. Keep in mind the past is gone, and the future is not here yet. This will help keep your thoughts in the moment and help you stay focused on your goals. Being mindful in the present moment and aware of what's happening in your present moment is important too.

6. Practice emotional self-control and increase your self-talk awareness, so you can begin to focus on the changes you desire. Make a personal commitment to yourself to own, embrace, and muster the courage and confidence to change the way you talk to and about yourself, and then take action.

Here are three quick tips for helping you manage your emotional state:

- Avoid reacting to difficult situations emotionally.
- Take a few deep breaths and focus on staying in the present moment.

- Practice positive self-talk, even when you're feeling down.

The word *unbelievable* carries a lot of weight. It has the power to shift our emotions from negative to positive in an instant. When we use this word to describe ourselves, it sends a powerful message to our subconscious mind that we are capable of anything. It inspires us to take action and reach for our goals.

7. Visualize yourself achieving your goals and living your dreams. Seeing yourself succeeding in your mind's eye is a powerful way to increase your chances of success in reality. Use relaxation techniques to help your mind achieve greater clarity as you bring greater focus to your intentions and the progress you are trying to make towards milestone goals.

Did you know that you have a wonderfully powerful tool onboard that you can use to propel yourself forward in the direction you want your life to shift toward? Your imagination! Unbelievable, eh?

By following these simple tips above and with a greater sense of self, you can dramatically improve the quality of your self-talk and, as a result, transform your life for the better. So start using positive, empowering self-talk today and watch your life change for the better.

Here's a final point, an important one to embrace in this process of self-improvement: Don't be afraid to show yourself some love and compassion. We all make mistakes, and we all have flaws. What matters is how we choose to view ourselves and our ability to learn from our mistakes. Be gentle with yourself, and always remember that you are worthy of love, respect, and happiness. Talk to yourself the way you would talk to a good friend, and watch your self-esteem and confidence soar! Watch for unbelievable improvements in how you think, feel, and act.

Remember, the words we use to describe ourselves have a direct impact on our self-image. You really do have more control over the trajectory of your life than you may have realized to this point. As stated earlier, as a reminder of something you already knew, words matter.

Remember, too, that it's never too late to start talking to yourself in a more positive and empowering way. The words you use today will shape your tomorrow. So choose wisely, and always speak kindly to and about yourself. You deserve nothing less.

Chapter 7:

Dissolving Self-Limiting Beliefs

Imagine going to your grave having carried unchecked, entirely false, completely untrue, and bogus negative beliefs that prevented you from living the prosperous, abundant, and joyful life you were meant to enjoy. It happens to people every day!! Yeah, I know. Unbelievable.

We all have them—those little voices in our heads that tell us we're not good enough, smart enough, or pretty enough. They're our self-limiting beliefs, and they can have a huge impact on our lives. It's not just our happiness that suffers; self-limiting beliefs can also prevent us from reaching our full potential. So how do we get rid of them?

Let's explore how to delete, dissolve, and remove self-limiting beliefs for good. Let's shift to empowerment!

Pat yourself on the back right now. I'll wait. Go ahead.

You are breaking a cycle by deciding to intervene, to interrupt a pattern that may have been handed down. Yes, future generations of your offspring will benefit from your decision in this moment, as you read this book, to take a stand and to end the crappy thinking that's in the way of you living a happier life!

Our subconscious mind power really is quite unbelievable, as Joseph Murphy and Émile Coué would both agree—something we touched on earlier in this book. We really are almost limitless when we actively manage and nurture our belief system, taking care to feed it properly with good, healthy thoughts. Asking our mind the right questions yields unbelievable results too. As both men also agreed, the subconscious mind is indeed programmable by ourselves and certainly by others wanting to alter our belief systems, our core values, and ultimately our actions and purchase decisions. Vigilance and loving care of our belief system is key!

When we get rid of self-limiting beliefs, we open ourselves up to a world of entirely new possibilities. It's almost as if the universe delivers them, and we can see the world from a new vantage point. We can achieve anything we set our minds to. So let's explore how to delete, dissolve, and remove self-limiting beliefs for good!

What Are Self-Limiting Beliefs Anyway?

Self-limiting beliefs are basically negative thoughts about ourselves that we've internalized over the years. They can come from a variety of sources, including our family, friends, society, and even the media. For example, you might believe that you're not good enough because your parents always told you that you needed to try harder. Or maybe you believe that you're not smart enough because you didn't do well in school. Whatever the source, self-limiting beliefs are harmful because they hold us back in life.

Self-limiting beliefs are nothing more than negative thoughts that we've allowed to take root in our minds. And like any negative thought, they can quickly spiral out of control if we're not careful. Left unchecked, self-limiting beliefs can become so deeply entrenched that it's hard to see anything else. They can color our perception of reality and prevent us from seeing the truth about ourselves and our potential.

Fortunately, there is a way to break free from the grip of self-limiting beliefs. It starts with language. The words we use to talk to ourselves can be incredibly powerful. They can either reinforce our self-limiting beliefs or help us let them go. In this blog post, we'll explore some of the language that can help us to delete, dissolve, and remove self-limiting beliefs from our lives so that we can start living the life we were meant to live.

How Do Self-Limiting Beliefs Limit Us?

Self-limiting beliefs limit us in a number of ways. First of all, they make us doubt ourselves and our ability to achieve our goals. Second, they cause us to "self-sabotage" by engaging in behaviors that are counterproductive to our success (such as procrastination or perfectionism). And last but not least, self-limiting beliefs can prevent us from taking risks and trying new things—which means we miss out on opportunities for growth and expansion.

False and limiting beliefs can prevent us from attaining our objectives or allow us to live our ideal lives. Fortunately, many psychological therapies include the ability to reverse these detrimental ideas, allowing us to begin living life as fully as possible. Hypnosis or self-hypnosis is a powerful tool in reframing our beliefs about ourselves and the world around us. When we shift our mindset to the present moment with optimism and hope, we can begin to release the negative beliefs that hold us back.

It's important to realize that self-limiting beliefs can have a negative impact on our lives in a number of ways. First, they can cause us to doubt ourselves in any area of life and in our ability to achieve our goals and intentions. Second, they can lead to self-sabotage by causing us to engage in behaviors that are counterproductive to our success. This is especially true if we're feeding our minds incorrect stories. And last but not least, self-limiting beliefs can prevent us from taking risks and trying new things, which means we miss out on opportunities for growth and expansion.

As Tony Robbins tells us about overcoming our limiting beliefs:

"When was the last time you gave up on something—and why? When was the last time you failed, and what did you tell yourself about the reason for your failure? If you told yourself anything other than 'I did my best and learned a lesson—and I will do better next time,' you're making excuses. You're letting limiting beliefs get in the way of achieving your goals. Overcoming limiting beliefs isn't always easy. They are deeply ingrained in us, often from childhood. But once you discover what they are and how to identify them, you can learn how to overcome your limiting beliefs. By incorporating actionable strategies for changing limiting beliefs into your everyday life, you can finally achieve everything you've ever dreamed of."

At a recent event I attended, the following Tony Robbins quote was shared with the group in the keynote session. Worth sharing here:

"The power of personal beliefs and the importance of controlling your state of mind: What you focus on expands. If you focus on the fact that you're broke, struggling, and failing, you'll get more of it. Further, we should constantly reexamine our beliefs about money,

business, 'what people will pay,' what you can do, etc. If you find yourself struggling in an area, I can practically guarantee you've got a disempowering, negative belief that's holding you back from being successful."

While the above pertains to business success, you can reframe it to have the right meaning as it applies to you. Let me pause you here to offer a few questions to help you examine your own situation:

1. Are you making excuses or telling your mind a story that sabotages yourself, perhaps without even realizing it?
2. Are you aware of the self-talk that feeds that story?
3. Are you feeling stuck or procrastinating on something important in your life because you are allowing false stories, excuses, or limiting beliefs stop you from what you truly want for yourself?

The answers are important! Let's get you unstuck!

As a professional hypnotist, I'm keenly aware of the impact that a negative self-belief can have on the quality of one's life or in the contribution of their life to their family, friends, community, or the world. Self-limiting beliefs are destructive thoughts that limit our potential and keep us from achieving our goals. They color our perception of reality and can prevent us from seeing the truth about ourselves and our potential.

What specific self-limiting beliefs are you harboring that just might be holding you back? Here are some of the most common self-limiting beliefs that hold others back:

1. I'm not good enough.

This is perhaps the most common self-limiting belief. People who believe this often feel that they're not smart enough, talented enough, or experienced enough to achieve their goals. As a result, they may not even attempt to pursue their dreams, as they feel that it's pointless. This belief can hold you back from achieving your goals and reaching your full potential.

2. I don't deserve it.

People who believe this often feel that they're not worthy of success or happiness. They may have low self-esteem or feel that they don't deserve good things in life. As a result, they may not take risks or put themselves in situations where they could potentially succeed. This self-limiting belief can prevent you from achieving success or reaching your goals. It's based on the idea that you're not worthy of success or happiness. This belief can be particularly damaging if it's based on past experiences or traumas.

3. It's too difficult.

Many people give up on their goals because they believe that achieving them is simply too difficult. They may feel that they don't have the skills or resources necessary to overcome the challenges involved. As a result, they may never even start working toward their goals. This belief can make you feel like giving up before you've even started. It can be especially difficult to overcome if you've already tried and failed at something in the past. This belief is often based on a fear of failure or a lack of confidence.

4. I don't have enough time.

Many people believe that they don't have enough time to achieve their goals. They may have other commitments, such as work or family, that take up a lot of their time and energy. As a result, they may never get around to working on their goals. This belief can make you feel like you'll never have enough time to achieve your dreams.

5. It's not possible.

Some people believe that their goals are simply not possible to achieve. They may feel that there are too many obstacles in their way or that the goal is too far out of reach. As a result, they may never even attempt to achieve their goal.

6. I'm not ready yet.

People who believe this often feel that they need more time to prepare before taking action toward their goal. They may want to wait until they have more knowledge or experience before starting to work toward it. As a result, they may never actually get started.

7 . Someone else will do it better than me.

Many people believe that someone else would be better suited to achieve their goal than themselves. They may feel that there's already someone who's more qualified or experienced than them. As a result, they might not bother trying to achieve the goal themselves.

8. I can't do it.

This self-limiting belief can prevent you from even trying to achieve your goals. If you believe that you can't do something, then you're likely to give up before you even start. This belief is often based on a fear of failure or a lack of confidence.

9. I'm not _____ enough.

This is a common self-limiting belief that can take on many different forms. People who believe this often feel that they are not _____ enough (fill in the blank). This could be smart enough, talented enough, experienced enough, etc. As a result, they may not attempt to achieve their goal. This belief can hold you back from achieving your potential.

10. It's not worth it.

People who believe this often feel that the effort required to achieve their goal is not worth the outcome. They may feel that it's not worth the time, energy, or money required to achieve their goal. As a result, they may never even start working toward their goal. This belief can make you feel like your goal is not worth pursuing.

11. I can't change.

This self-limiting belief is based on the idea that we're stuck in our current situation and that change is impossible. This belief can prevent us from taking any action toward our goals or making any positive changes in our lives. It can make us feel like we're powerless to change our circumstances.

12. I am not lovable, not worthy of love and respect.

This self-limiting belief can prevent us from seeking out love and intimacy. It can make us feel like we're not worthy of love and affection. As a result, we may never experience the close relationships that we desire.

How to Remove Self-Limiting Beliefs

Before jumping into the process, let me share briefly a couple of important concepts that I utilize with clients at my hypnotherapy practice. Embracing these two points with your fullness of being and your belief that you can do anything you put your mind to doing will push the limiting beliefs right out of your life.

- Where our attention goes is where the energy flows. Focus on what you want in life rather than what you don't want to experience more of. Set an intention, visualize it, and connect to it. Own it. Believe it. Achieve it.

- Learn from the past, live in the present with an eye on what the future may bestow, reveal, or deliver as a result of your optimism and your deliberate actions toward your intentions.

The first step is to become aware of your self-limiting beliefs. A lot of times, we're not even aware of the negative thoughts we have about ourselves—but once you start paying attention, you'll be surprised at how often these thoughts pop up. Once you've identified your self-limiting beliefs, the next step is to question them. Why do you believe these things about yourself? Where did they come from? Are they really true?

The Language of Deletion

A truly big commitment is required here, and baby steps are perfectly fine. This is a process that begins with you. Your journey toward greatness begins now. Decide right now that you are destined for greater things in life; more joy, more abundance, greater happiness, and certainly more prosperity. Decide that it's time for you to make the shift toward developing more empowering beliefs. Decide that you are unstoppable and that you can do anything you put your mind to doing!

One of the most effective ways to deal with self-limiting beliefs is to simply delete them from your life. Just like you would delete a harmful virus from your computer, you need to delete these negative thoughts from your mind. And you can do that by using what I call "the language of deletion."

To get rid of self-limiting beliefs, you can use a special kind of language that deletes them from your mind. Just say to yourself, "I delete this belief from my mind," and it will be gone! Say, "I simply refuse to accept these limiting beliefs that are holding me back."

Here are some examples of phrases you can use to delete self-limiting beliefs from your life:

- "I am not my self-limiting belief." This phrase helps you to separate yourself from the negative thought. You are not your self-limiting belief; it is something that is happening TO you, not something that is a part of who you are. This simple shift in perspective can be incredibly empowering.
- "I am deleting all self-limiting beliefs from my life." This phrase is a declaration of war on your negative thoughts. It's a way of saying, "I'm done with these harmful thoughts; they no longer have any power over me."
- "I am dissolving all self-limiting beliefs now." This phrase helps visualize the process of letting go of these negative thoughts. See them being dissolved into nothingness, unable to reconstitute from this state.

After you've questioned your self-limiting beliefs and decided that they are indeed false, it's time to let them go. One way to do this is by replacing them with positive affirmations such as "I am capable," or "I am worthy," or "I am deserving of love and happiness." You can also try visualization exercises in which you imagine yourself achieving your goals despite your self-doubt. The more you practice affirming and visualizing, the easier it will be to let go of those harmful self-limiting beliefs for good.

Mindset, Attitude, and Language Help Shape Your Belief System

Of course, our life's experiences, especially our childhood, also shape our beliefs. It's important to examine and validate or change some of them!

It's unbelievable when you stop to think about it. We do have the power of our awesome mind to help us through any situation. Choosing to be calm, relaxed, and in control of our emotions is usually a good first step in navigating through anything.

Launching Your Empowering Beliefs

Whether we realize it or not, our beliefs have the ability to bring about both positive and negative outcomes. So what exactly is a belief? It's simply defined as a feeling of certainty with regard to the meaning of something. The issue is that most of our core beliefs were established long ago based on past experiences that caused us either pain or pleasure. Are you starting to feel the power of the word *unbelievable*?

The past, however, does not determine the present—unless you continue to reside there. Experiences may be found to support almost any conviction if we are merely conscious of our beliefs. Is it true that your ideas do not empower you? Change them if necessary. Will your ideas be the reason you cease taking action toward the outcomes you desire in life? Or will you modify them into the chance to create something world-class—whether it's a personal revolution, a career development, or a family change?

It is always your choice.

You can choose to believe that you are powerless and at the mercy of fate, or you can choose to believe that you have the power to create your own destiny. The empowering belief is that you are in control of your life; you have the ability to make things happen. This doesn't mean that you won't experience adversity or setbacks—everyone does. But it does mean that you have the inner strength and fortitude to overcome any obstacle. Use positive affirmations to stay in the zone—that circle of excellence.

The first step to creating empowering beliefs is to become aware of your current belief system, as already discussed. What do you believe about yourself, your abilities, and your potential? Do these beliefs inspire you to take action and achieve your goals? If not, it's time for a change.

Remember, you can choose what you believe, so choose wisely. The beliefs you hold about yourself will either limit or empower you. It's up to you to decide which it will be.

Self-limiting beliefs can have a major impact on our lives, but it doesn't have to be this way. By becoming aware of our negative thoughts and questioning their validity, we can begin to let go of these harmful belief systems and replace them with positive affirmations. With practice, it will become easier and easier to achieve our goals without letting self-doubt hold us back.

Keep in mind that self-limiting beliefs have no place in a life lived to its fullest potential. They limit our ability to see ourselves clearly and prevent us from achieving our goals. But by using language deliberately and with intention, we can delete, dissolve, and remove these harmful thoughts so that they no longer have any power over us. When we do this, we open ourselves up to limitless possibilities and begin living the life we were meant to live.

Take these ten famous quotes "to the bank" and begin to adopt the same joie de vivre!

1. "Believe in yourself and all that you are. Know that there is something inside you that is greater than any obstacle." —Christian Larson

2. "Your belief becomes your reality."—Tony Robbins

3. "Whatever the mind can conceive and believe, it can achieve."—Napoleon Hill

4. "I can, therefore I am."—Simone Weil

5. "If you want to live a happy life, tie it to a goal, not to people or things."—Albert Einstein

6. "The only limit to our realization of tomorrow will be our doubts of today."—Franklin D. Roosevelt

7. "We must let go of the life we have planned, so as to accept the one that is waiting for us."—Joseph Campbell

8. "The question isn't who is going to let me; it's who is going to stop me."—Ayn Rand

9. "People often say that motivation doesn't last. Well, neither does bathing. That's why we recommend it daily."—Zig Ziglar

10. "If you can dream it, you can do it."—Walt Disney

Chapter 8:

Relaxing into That New You

"No matter how much pressure you feel at work, if you could find ways to relax for at least five minutes every hour, you'd be more productive."
—Dr. Joyce Brothers

You may begin to notice, as you become more masterful and more comfortable with your increased speaking confidence. You may have already noticed an increased awareness of your feelings of contentment in your communication efforts.

After all, you are becoming more courageous and more charismatic, too!

You'll observe this about yourself, as well: you are more relaxed in situations where you once felt uncomfortable or avoided altogether! Unbelievable!

While it's true that relaxation isn't required to achieve hypnotic influence and success, I do teach it to every client who comes into my office. I teach them how to relax their mind and body so they can condition themselves to live a calmer, more in control, and more emotionally mature experience each day.

You are already unbelievable, yet there is a new you emerging each and every day. Small incremental steps propel you forward at your pace and advance you toward greatness. Awesome, unbelievable things lie ahead. Keep it up!

An essential key to unlocking that awesomeness, that evolving and emerging greatness that shows itself each day, if even in a small way, is in learning how to relax deeply—to achieve that profoundly deep restful state, as my colleague Joseph Onesta would say, even in your awakened state!

Taking a break from the hustle and bustle of life can have incredible impacts on your well-being. Here are some reasons to de-stress:

1. Taking time for yourself helps you stay focused, organized, and clear-minded.
2. Relaxing is like pressing pause—it will help slow down your heart rate, reduce blood pressure levels, and keep tension away!

3. It also aids digestion by helping you absorb essential nutrients easier, which in turn fights diseases and infection better than before!

4. You'll thank yourself later as it improves sleeping cycles with an increase in endorphins and serotonin!

The Relaxation Response is the Key!

If you want to live a more consistently calm, serenely authentic life, then learn how to invoke the relaxation response, which Dr. Herbert Benson coined in 1975 but which I am confident has been known for millennia.

Invoking the Relaxation Response

The relaxation response is included here because I want you to master it. It is key to your consistently improving sleep experience, as it is useful during your pre-sleep rituals and when you crawl into bed. Sorry, I know I've mentioned the importance of relaxation previously, but it bears repeating, and I cannot underscore it enough. Allow me to go into it in a little more detail here, if you will, and don't be at all surprised if I bring the subject of relaxation up again later on in the book as well.

Fight, flight, or freeze! These responses are our survival instincts, coded into our genes and passed down to us by our ancestors. If there were a tiger at the door (or at the entrance to our cave), for instance, roaring and banging to get in, when presented with the tiger, we are either going to freeze, run, or stand and fight the animal.

As *Harvard Health* explains, "First described by Dr. Walter B. Cannon at Harvard Medical School in the 1920s, the fight-or-flight response evolved as a survival mechanism. When we encounter a life-threatening situation, a surge of stress hormones prepares us to fight or to flee."

It's an automatic response that causes temporary stress. Our body reacts to what we are sensing, thinking, and feeling and responds. Our heart beats faster, muscles contract, adrenaline flows, arteries constrict, and we are ready to take one of those three survival responses. Sometimes, that stress response lingers. Usually, it subsides as the danger fades, but sometimes we cannot turn it off without conscious intervention. Sometimes the stress or anxiety "program" keeps playing, and we forget to realize we can turn it off.

We can calm the stress response, however, by consciously reversing the body's reaction to the perceived feelings of danger. Dr. Herbert Benson, in his 1975 book *The Relaxation Response*, taught the modern world how to do just this, and his Benson-Henry Institute for Mind Body Medicine at Massachusetts General Hospital has been focused on the science and methods of deep relaxation. Dr. Benson, one of the world's first Western physicians to bring spirituality and mind–body healing into medicine, coined the term "relaxation response" in a 1974 article in the medical journal *Psychiatry*. At that time, he noted that such practices as Zen meditation, yoga, repetitive prayer, progressive muscle relaxation, and even hypnosis could invoke measurable physiological changes. Relaxation was measurable. In fact, this author (yours truly, Bob Martel) recently underwent electromyographic nerve testing (EMG) for a pinched nerve and was able to use self-hypnosis to show the neurologist that the relaxation response I consciously triggered had removed the measurable muscle tension in my arm. Ah, the power of the mind!

Using this relaxation technique will prepare you for better sleep and for better performance throughout the day! The relaxation response is defined as "the response that is the opposite of the fight-or-flight or stress response." Based on widely known practices that have been used for millennia, the relaxation response is very similar in many ways to prayer, meditation, and repetitive motion techniques, such as those referred to as bilateral stimulation.

Eliciting the relaxation response takes only a few moments and builds resiliency in mind and body, helps the immune system, and creates a feeling of control over emotions. And it also, in plain words, just makes you feel so damn relaxed!

When we practice the relaxation response, which you are about to learn, the body becomes more physiologically relaxed. Blood pressure is lowered, blood flow is increased, oxygen to the blood is optimized, and hormones return to normal levels. Over the past few decades, as Benson explains in his latest book on the subject, *The Relaxation Revolution*, the technique has been proven effective in many ways, including lowering blood pressure, as cited in his 1974 study published in *The Lancet*, and in aiding in reducing or eliminating insomnia.

The relaxation response is easy to learn and practice. Too many meditation gurus complicate the process. It is merely a matter of breathing and focusing and can be accomplished in a matter of moments. With the addition of an anchor or two to connect your intention to a feeling, you can shift from the stress–fear state to a calm and relaxed state, invoking the exact opposite of the stress response. Keep it simple, and you cannot fail at this!

Practicing the relaxation response on a regular basis is transformational. It is a time set aside for you to shift from the busy pace of life and to pause and be present with yourself, sitting quietly and still. This allows your mind and body to restore, focusing simply on the breath or on a selected word such as "calm" or "relaxed."

Now, with that said, realize that there is no one way to practice the relaxation response successfully. It's all about focus and breaking the train of everyday thought to, in Benson's words, "evoke this physiological state." Before I walk you through the technique, let me share a few examples of people deliberately immersed in the relaxation response:

The bingo hall filled with people dabbing their sheets, some with their good luck charms and trolls by their side, moving their arms in unison to the caller's numbers, focused intently on calling "bingo!" when their number is shouted out. They are in the zone.

The person practicing yoga or Tai Chi in a class or in front of the TV with their at-home video classes. They are in the zone, too, focused on the movements and the instructions from their teacher.

The person practicing their musical instrument or singing in the shower. Focused, relaxed, in the zone.

The athlete on the gridiron, the ballfield, the tennis court, or the lacrosse field — focused on relaxing into the process of enjoying playing their chosen sport. In the zone.

The person feeling stress and anxiety who can practice what you will learn next to consciously invoke Dr. Benson's technique. You'll be in the zone, and further, you'll be able to instantly call up that relaxed state using your new self-hypnosis techniques, too!

Here is one technique for invoking the relaxation response. It is based on Benson's basic guidance, and it can be the foundation for innumerable strategies to relax deeply. Paraphrasing his explanation:

1) Select a repetitive thought upon which you can focus while disregarding other thoughts when they come to mind. It's easier than you might think and just requires a little mind conditioning. I am confident you'll get the hang of it.

a. Let's use the words "calm" and "relax."

b. You could also choose a word like "peace" or "love," as Benson also suggests.

c. You could choose a faith-based anchor word or phrase such as "Jesus," "Hail Mary/Ave Maria," "Shalom," or other peaceful spiritual words for your faith or phrases that reset your mind in this direction.

2) As Benson suggests, if other thoughts float to the surface while attempting to relax and focus, simply say, "Oh well," and without judgment or criticism, be aware of it and let it float away as you bring your attention back to your intention.

3) Sit comfortably, close your eyes, and take a deep, relaxing breath—the best breath you can take. In through your nose, hold it for a few seconds, and exhale

through your mouth. Now again, and as you do so, say your chosen word or phrase to yourself silently as you breathe in again and exhale again, being sure to take a full belly breath and pausing before you exhale, allowing for a full exchange of oxygen into your lungs and carbon dioxide out.

4) Take a moment to double-check your comfort position. Relax all the muscles in your body: your feet, up your legs to your hips, further up and up to your core, your neck and shoulders, your arms. Let your entire face and jaw relax. Breathe again, saying your chosen word or phrase.

5) Expect and anticipate other thoughts to emerge. Simply usher them along and stay focused on your breathing.

6) Breathe and relax for four to five minutes.

7) Now, with that relaxation response in place, keep your eyes closed as you begin to emerge now, allowing your regular thoughts to return. And then slowly open your eyes.

8) Sit for a moment with your eyes open before getting back up.

Practice relaxation daily. I cannot stress this enough. Decide it's a skill worth living as it could indeed change the very course of your life. Have courage enough to go there!

Anchor it or connect it to a word, a breath, or even by touching your thumb and finger together, making a circle. Take a few cleansing deep breaths as you do this, and say: *I am calm, I am relaxed, I am in control*, followed by another deep breath. With practice, you can create a conditioned response enabling you to access your deepest most relaxed state. Try it. Unbelievable.

> "Calm mind brings inner strength and self-confidence, so that's very important for good health."
> —Dalai Lama

It's best if you can find a small bit of time in the morning, before breakfast perhaps, for five minutes or so, after dinner for five minutes, and also for a few minutes during your new pre-sleep habitual rituals you're embracing on this journey. Later, we'll talk about anchoring your relaxed state to a cue that you can use throughout your day and prior to sleep.

As I mentioned and as Benson emphasizes, there are many ways to accomplish relaxation. For our purposes, the above works quite well. It is something I teach all my clinical hypnosis clients to do! Now it's your turn to practice it! Dr. Benson's original book, *The Relaxation Response*, and his newer book, *Relaxation Revolution: The Science and Genetics of Mind Body Healing* are valuable resources, and both belong on your bookshelf. Make a note of it, as I want you to do your best and stay on track.

"Learn to relax. Your body is precious, as it houses your mind and spirit. Inner peace begins with a relaxed body."
—Norman Vincent Peale

Chapter 9:

The Magic of Your Brain and the RAS as a Programmable Filter

"The human brain is a funny thing: it's very susceptible to tempo and melody. You put the right words to it, and it becomes very influential."
—Ray Stevens, singer, songwriter

Don't think of a pink elephant!

Sorry, that was unfair. I just tapped into your brain's reticular activating system (RAS) and made you think of a pink elephant.

Hypnotists do this all the time! When I have a smoker in the office, I will say while they are focused on being a nonsmoker, "I want you to vividly imagine the color red. Any shade and anywhere; a stop sign, brake lights, a truck, a car, a radish, nail polish, or a blouse. Let it be a subconscious and automatic reminder that you are a nonsmoker and will remain a nonsmoker for the rest of your life."

A tap into their subconscious mind's RAS!

I may also ask them as an example, "Have you ever bought a new car or new pair of shoes, and you start seeing it everywhere you turn? That's the RAS working." And, so apropos to our discussion and this very book, I also use the example of "Do you ever learn of a new word and start hearing that word everywhere?" Unbelievable, eh?

Speaking of the word *don't*. When we use it as above, it causes the brain to focus on what comes after it. It often has a reverse effect. Be aware.

The RAS is the reason you learn a new word, and then start hearing it everywhere. It's why you can tune out of a crowd of talking people yet immediately snap to attention when someone says your name or something that at least sounds like it. Please note, however, that my discussion of the RAS only scratches the surface insofar as it prepares you to be a highly influential "operator" of others' attention. I've included it to call your attention (tapping your RAS again!) to the importance of understanding the how and why of the power of your words.

A basic understanding of the RAS is important because your words activate it! When you use the word *unbelievable* in conversation, you are inducing a hypnotic, automatic response by the RAS.

Read on!

As Chase Hughes, neuroscientist and behavioral influence expert, says in a recent discussion in his applied behavior research group:

> "The brain is like a computer and is regularly programmed to run specific scripts. When your mind is told (by you or someone else) that something is important, you will notice it at a higher rate. This is done out of necessity as it would be overwhelming to absorb every single sight, sound, and smell that crosses your path. So, your subconscious protects you from what it labels as unimportant. The cool thing about this feature of the brain is that you can use it to your advantage. Want to find more opportunities? Program your mind to look for them. Want to find more beauty in the world? Program your mind to notice beautiful things around you. Want to find more inspiration? Program your mind to seek stories, people, and words that inspire you. There isn't a limit on the types of things you can program your mind to seek. The risk though is if you inadvertently focus on things you fear, dislike, or want to avoid, your subconscious can be programmed to notice more of those things. The choice is yours. Choose wisely."

When I explain RAS to people, I tell them it's like a programmable filter. The reticular activating system comprises an extensive portion of the brain stem. Think of it as an awesomely powerful mind tool within your body that you can direct; simply by the power of your intentions. Our intentions create our reality, and when your intention is to sleep, your RAS will assist you when your intentions are congruent with your behavior. In other words, your mind and body are looking for alignment, matching your thoughts, feelings, imagery, and actions. It prompts your awareness to search for specifics that are meaningful to you. The reticular formation is the part of the brain that determines what you pay attention to throughout the day.

The RAS is a bundle of nerves that sits at the base of your brain stem. It starts above your spinal cord and is about two inches long. It's about the width of a pencil, and it's where all your senses come into play. Well, except for your smell, which goes into the emotional center of your brain, but the rest of them come in through the RAS, and what the RAS does is really connect that subconscious part of our brain with the conscious part of our brain. The words you hear and those you hear silently in your mind resonate and influence the RAS.

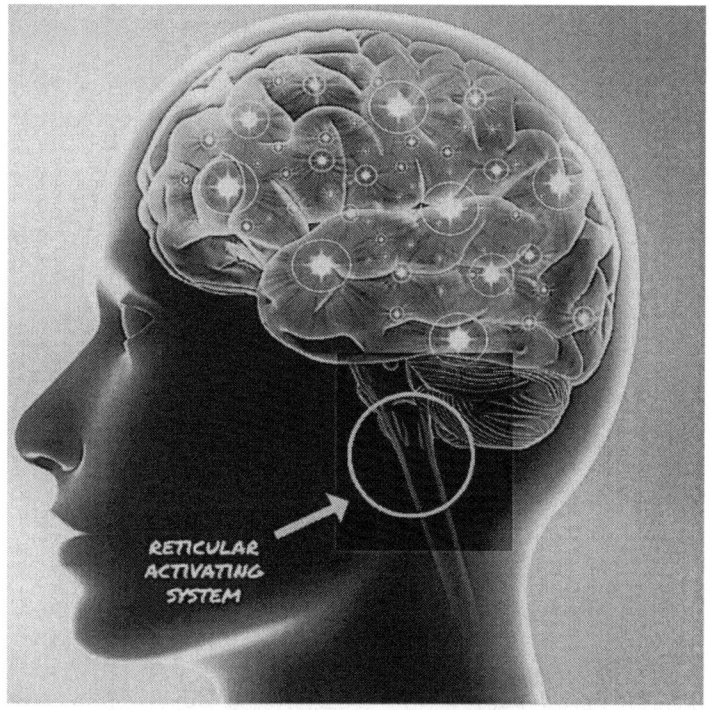

Figure 1: Reticular activating system (RAS)

Said another way, the RAS is responsible for our wakefulness, ability to focus, and fight or flight response. It helps us to perceive the world around us. The RAS acts as a gatekeeper between our conscious and unconscious mind.The reticular activating system is a part of the brain. It starts near the top of the spinal column and goes up around two inches. It is slightly wider than a pencil. All of your senses go to this bundle of neurons, which is about the size of your little finger.

As I share with clients or when I speak on the subject and at the risk of sounding redundant here:

"The primary role of the RAS is regulating arousal and awake–asleep transitions. Without launching into a course on neuroscience, it helps to be aware that your sleep routine impacts your RAS, and more importantly, you can take action by the choices you make and the changes you decide to undertake when it comes to preparing for sleep. The RAS is involved in our fight or flight responses to the sense of fear, and it can become overactive by such things as post-traumatic stress, excessive worry, and your focus on negativity. The RAS controls your sleeping patterns and may become unregulated or overstimulated, which in turn, makes it difficult to get to sleep and remain in the sleep state. The RAS is important for many different functions, like controlling your sleep, wakefulness, and attention. It also helps you process information and make decisions. Without the RAS, you would not be able to function properly."

Here's What's Important to Know

By understanding how the RAS works, we can use it to our advantage. By training ourselves to become more aware of its effects and using these methods to regulate our arousal levels, we can increase our alertness and productivity. In turn, this can help us achieve our goals and live a more successful life. It can also impact others, especially our words. So it's important to stay conscious of the effects our words have on those around us.

Here's What's Important To Know About the RAS

The RAS is responsible for determining what you notice and experience in the world. The senses that the RAS uses to do this are:

- Sight: visualized in reality or imagination
- Sound (including internal thoughts and words)
- Taste
- Touch

For example, maybe you've been in a noisy restaurant but were still able to focus on the conversation you're having. That's your RAS working hard to filter out unimportant noise.

Your RAS works with your limbic system and prefrontal cortex to determine what information is important enough to pay attention to. It's why you can remember a phone number or why you know how to drive without thinking about it. With the right intention and focus, you can tap into the power of the RAS.

For example, you can create affirmations that are positively charged and focus your RAS on what you want. When your subconscious hears affirmation after affirmation about something positive, eventually, it will start to believe it's true. This means that by using the power of the RAS, you have control over how you think and perceive yourself.

Unbelievable, eh? You bet! We were designed this way.

The vagus nerve is a part of the RAS. It's responsible for transmitting signals from the brain stem to the thalamus, which then sends sensory information to the rest of the nervous system. The RAS helps filter what you take in and pay attention to, as well as activate parts of your body and brain during sleep and wakefulness. The vagus nerve is a key part of this process, enabling the filtering of sensory information, regulating your level of alertness, and controlling reflexive muscle responses. It also helps regulate breathing, heart rate, digestion, and other body functions. In summary, the vagus nerve plays an important role in helping your RAS filter sensory information and maintain your level of alertness.

What can you do to activate or control the RAS?

Good or bad, positive or negative, whatever we focus on becomes real for us. I believe that we are abundance-seeking souls here on this planet and that God wants us all to enjoy great abundance, joy, fulfillment, prosperity, and happiness. It's a journey.

We have the ability to use our free will to make better choices, and knowing that the RAS plays such a key role in our destiny, why not take an active role in programming it (instead of letting others do it for us)? Of course, deep down at the DNA level, our RAS is programmed to help us survive, as in the flight or flight fear response, for example.

If you spend your time dwelling on the negative, all you will attract is more negativity. Conversely, if you focus on the positive, good things will come your way because that's what your brain is hardwired to do. This isn't magic; it's how our RAS works.

There are several ways to activate your RAS. One way is to focus on a specific goal or intention, as this will help the RAS filter out distractions and bring more attention to the goal. Additionally, engaging in activities that stimulate all five senses can help activate the RAS and increase alertness. Examples of such activities include yoga and meditation, listening to music or nature sounds, practicing aromatherapy, eating healthy foods with different textures and flavors, and even just being more mindful throughout your day. Finally, getting adequate rest and taking time for yourself can also help you activate your RAS.

Sometimes we feel overwhelmed, unfocused, and just plain stuck. But know that we can indeed program our mind for success. If we set our goal and refocus, however, our RAS might help us out. Our brains always look after what benefits us the most. Our RAS is constantly filtering through an abnormal amount of data so that we can see and hear and be whoever or whatever we want to be. Sounds quite like a superpower if you ask me.

By activating the RAS, you can become more aware of your environment and have better focus on the tasks at hand. Doing so will help you live a life that is more mindful, productive, and satisfying.

How does the RAS affect mental health?

The RAS plays an important role in regulating our level of alertness and attention, as well as filtering out unnecessary sensory information. Therefore, when the RAS is functioning optimally, it can help improve mental health. It can help us stay focused on important tasks, allow us to better process our feelings, and reduce stress. Additionally, by activating the RAS through activities that stimulate all five senses, we can increase alertness and improve well-being. This will enable us to become more mindful of our environment and take better care of ourselves. Ultimately, a healthy RAS can help us be more productive, relaxed, and content.

What are the benefits of a healthy RAS?

There are many benefits to having a healthy RAS. A healthy RAS can help us become more aware of our environment, maintain focus on important tasks, and better process sensory information. This can help us be more mindful of our feelings and take better care of ourselves. Additionally, by activating the RAS through activities that stimulate all five senses, we can increase alertness and reduce stress. Ultimately, a healthy RAS enables us to live more productive lives with improved mental health.

You might find this to be true or a real stretch. I believe that the RAS is the part of us with which God communicates with us in prayer or even through thoughts that we may not be able to fully explain, such as a calling. After all, if we can train our RAS based on our set intentions and the words we choose to use to lead us toward what we visualize, well, can't the spoken or written words of God do the same? I think so.

One way to do this, as recommended by author, consultant, and marketing genius Perry Marshall: "Get in the habit of reading one Psalm each morning. By focusing your mind on scripture, you are simply programming your RAS to hear the word of God as it relates to your life."

If we're not careful, these same principles of RAS programming can work against us. Train your RAS to focus on confirmation bias instead of reliable evidence. For example, if you imagine going to your job and everyone hating you, it will feel like this is true because that's the information your brain is focusing on. Similarly, if you consistently tell yourself you'll get nervous around a person or event, then when you actually experience it next, it will seem more likely your brain will believe this about yourself and act accordingly. Whatever we believe is true, right? Sometimes we need to shift what we believe.

Activating the RAS either in hypnosis or self-hypnosis is also the key to allowing our subconscious mind to hear, embrace, and accept healthy suggestions for our highest and best, based on our intentions.

The RAS also controls how you perceive yourself and your quality of life. It plays a key function in the state of our self-image. When it is functioning optimally, you can be more confident and secure in yourself. This can result in a greater sense of self-esteem and fulfillment, allowing you to take on life's challenges without feeling overwhelmed. A healthy RAS can also lead to improved relationships with others as well as increased motivation and productivity. Ultimately, having a healthy RAS can be an invaluable asset to leading a happier and more successful life.

The RAS is responsible for the beliefs you hold in your brain. Your RAS looks to make those beliefs a reality. This can have a big influence on how you understand and experience the world around you. It's crucial to comprehend how your RAS works as well as ways to keep healthy levels of activation in order to optimize mental clarity, focus, productivity, and well-being entirely. By gaining an understanding of your RAS, you can help guarantee that you live a life full of purpose with intention focused on things that matter to you most.

When it comes to activating your RAS, the key is to become aware of your environment and start implementing small changes in your daily routine. By doing so, you can begin to experience a greater level of clarity in your thoughts, more focus in your work, and improved productivity in all areas of your life. Additionally, making these changes can also lead to increased satisfaction with your life overall. So, what are some small changes you can start making today?

Advertisers use the RAS to make you more aware of their product. You can do the same thing by being mindful of what you're looking for and setting intentions to find it. For example, if you need a new pair of jeans, set an intention to find the perfect fit or style. This will help focus your attention on certain stores or brands that carry what you're looking for, and the RAS will have an easier time bringing you what you're wanting.

Now you have more than you need on the topic of the RAS. Hopefully, I have given you insights into the power of your own thoughts and intentions and the unbelievable impact your words have on others! Unbelievable!

So why is understanding the RAS really so important?

As Chase Hughes says in his best-selling book, *The Ellipsis Manual*, the first step in influence is to command the focused attention of those you are trying to impact. Says Hughes, on p. 174:

> "When a subject becomes focused on a conversation, the slight shifts in your behavior allow further building of advanced compliance and assist in the achievement of your outcome."

In other words, once you gain focused attention from the other party or group of people, it's then that your opportunity to achieve influential success begins. As I said in the second sentence of this book's introduction, using the word *unbelievable* will help you establish focused attention quickly.

In fact, as Chase Hughes also says in *The Ellipsis Manual*, pp. 175–77, "Focus, interest, and curiosity are the building blocks of influence." Paraphrasing his exact words; once you have focus, deeper attention, interest, and curiosity will more easily follow.

Now, take a look at the sample sentences that follow, offered in Part Two.

Part Two:

Examples of Unbelievable Phrases to Test-Drive Immediately

The following phrases are offered to illustrate examples of the word *unbelievable* being woven into the conversation. Of course, there are unlimited uses, but this should get you started. Use these or similar phrases in your own self-talk to program your mind for positivity and success. Use them in conversations with others or in your writing to literally program the reticular activating system (RAS) in the brains of your listeners!

As you may recall from the previous chapter, the RAS is a programmable filter that impacts what the mind focuses on or tunes into and can be anchored to a response in the present moment or in the future.

For example, in my hypnotherapy practice, I tell my smoking cessation clients:

"As you continue to shift to a deeper place and allow your open mind to hear new suggestions, you might find this unbelievable. I want you to vividly picture in your mind the color red. It could be a deep red, a light red, a stop sign, a taillight on a car or truck. Any time now, for the next two to three weeks, any time at all, the color red, red, red will be an automatic, subconscious reminder that you are a nonsmoker and will remain a nonsmoker for the rest of your life."

See how I used the word *unbelievable* to set up what's coming next?

Let me try that once more for you:

"As you begin to wonder what changes lie ahead with your new focus on this word and, more importantly, on your new lexical superpowers, get ready for some unbelievable responses from people. You'll be surprised to see how people gravitate toward you or how they simply make room for your contribution in a conversation."

As you read these phrases, begin thinking how you might apply them to your life or how you might modify them to fit. They are presented in no particular order of importance. Some examples are provided, especially where I want to point out powerful uses!

Keep in mind the following key points:

- Tonality matters in communications. Be aware of where you put the emphasis in the words you choose and in how you say *unbelievable.* Be deliberate, and check your emotional state.
- Your intention and your message. This underlies your message.
- Delivery of the message. The speed of spoken words and your pauses and inflections all impact the message.

When you say *unbelievable,* mean it in the context of your desired outcome.

Remember this always. Be sincere and ethical in your intentions. Good will come of it.

Enjoy!

1. I am unbelievable!

    Try this on for size. Shift into a positive mind state. Deep breath and a big smile. Say to yourself: "I am <first name>. I am okay, and I am truly unbelievable." Breathe, relax, and repeat. Program your mind to adopt a new self-enabling belief! You could even add the affirmation: "I am enough, and I unconditionally love and accept myself." Try it.

2. You are unbelievable!

    This phrase can be used to deliver a nice compliment or to give either positive or negative feedback to someone. Keep in mind that with effort and careful word choices, you can deliver negative feedback positively.

For example: "Honey, you are unbelievable. Thank you for surprising me with that awesome dinner."

3. He/She is unbelievable!

"You know, Martha. I was in the front row when Steve gave that presentation. You had to be there to see it. He is absolutely unbelievable in front of a crowd. From my standpoint, his message was well received."

4. Well, isn't that just unbelievable?

"So, Johnny, you got picked to be in the school play. Isn't that unbelievable? You said you'd never get picked and look at that! Wow!"

5. Honey, that's unbelievable.

Keeping one eye on the football game on TV and one ear listening to his wife's conversation and issuing a few yups and ahas, he finally said *unbelievable* to whatever she was saying.

6. In response to any question: Unbelievable!

"That is an unbelievable question." Or "It's rather unbelievable that I have not yet been asked that question. Can I get back to you on that?"

7. That's flipping unbelievable!

   "Can you imagine what was just reported on the news about the price of gasoline? That's flipping unbelievable."

8. "How was the traffic, dear?"

   "Un-freaking-believable."

   No matter the traffic was heavy or there weren't any cars on the road, it's the correct response.

9. I had an unbelievable dinner experience last night.

10. Answering a question.

    "You know, it was almost too unbelievable to even imagine. It was (great, lousy, beyond expectations, etc.)."

11. "What an amazing sunrise. Simply unbelievable."

12. "You look amazingly unbelievable in that dress."

13. "And your smile completes the outfit. Truly unbelievably stunning."

14. "I felt really unbelievable coming out of church yesterday."

15. "I feel unbelievably more in control of my emotions than I have felt in a long time."

16. "Simply unbelievable. Yes, I feel unbelievably confident and courageous today."

17. "How was your trip?"

"I'm tired from the journey, but the trip was unbelievable."

18. "It's unbelievable how people drive today."

19. "I had an unbelievable hike this past weekend. I needed that walk in the woods."

20. "I feel unbelievable right now."

21. "You are unbelievably talented. Glad you are on our team!"

22. "I feel incredibly unbelievable. I swear I slept at a Holiday Inn Express."

23. Answering "How you doing?"

"I feel unbelievable."

Answering "How you doing?"

"I feel positively unbelievable."

24. Answering "How is business?"

"Unbelievable."

Author's Final Thoughts

Thank you for reading this book!

Just as it was for Peter, whom I mentioned early in the book, I hope that shifting your vocabulary leads to greater success and new adventures. Adopting the word *unbelievable* into his daily lexicon really strengthened his confidence, and he mustered up the courage to pursue his acting career.

His story was the motivation for the book in your hands now. His courage and confidence opened new doors for him. My hope is that your increased confidence will lead to greater courage and even greater success. Shifting your self-talk and the words you use in conversation with others will have a profoundly positive impact on your life and perhaps on theirs too!

I encourage you to experiment and develop a short list of similar attention-getting words.

I welcome your feedback and your stories. I'm very interested to know how adding *unbelievable* impacts your life! If I can be of any help as a hypnotist or coach, please reach out to bob@bobmartel.com.

About the Author

Robert Martel is a professional clinical hypnotist in private practice at Positive Results Hypnosis in Holden, MA, which he founded in 2008. Bob is also a performance and confidence coach to business professionals and athletes who want to take their game in business or in life to the next level. He is a certified NLP practitioner and life coach through the ICBCH. Bob also founded a direct marketing consulting group in 1992, where he specialized in direct marketing and copywriting, serving clients in numerous industries using hypnotic influence and persuasion techniques to help clients profitably grow their businesses. He provides clinical hypnosis services at his office and over the internet, serving clients worldwide.

As America's leading hypnotic sleep coach, Bob has worked with thousands of people to help them sleep better, enabling them to live happier, more abundant, and joyful lives by using the power of their minds to connect with their God-given talents and gifts.

He is a graduate of Northeastern University and a veteran of the U.S. Navy's submarine service. He is certified by the ICBCH as an NLP practitioner and life coach and is an ICBCH and NGH-certified hypnosis instructor. He is also board certified by the National Guild of Hypnotists. Bob is a commercial hot-air balloon pilot and resides in Central Massachusetts.

Do you want Bob to speak at your next event, provide private coaching, or conduct a customized program for your company or your team? Call (508) 481-8383, visit www.positiveresultshypnosis.com, email him at Bob@bobmartel.com, or visit his LinkedIn profile at LinkedIn.com/in/robertmartel

Made in the USA
Monee, IL
10 June 2026

53029989R00077